The New Challenge of
Direct Democracy

For Robert A. Dahl
teacher, supervisor and inspiration
for two generations of democratic theorists

The New Challenge of Direct Democracy

Ian Budge

Polity Press

The right of Ian Budge to be identified as author of this work has been asserted in accordance with the Copyright, Designs and Patents Act 1988.

First published in 1996 by Polity Press in association with Blackwell Publishers Ltd.

2 4 6 8 9 10 7 5 3 1

Editorial office:
Polity Press
65 Bridge Street
Cambridge CB2 1UR, UK

Marketing and production:
Blackwell Publishers Ltd
108 Cowley Road
Oxford OX4 1JF, UK

Published in the USA by
Blackwell Publishers Inc.
238 Main Street
Cambridge, MA 02142, USA

ISBN 0-7456-1231-8
ISBN 0-7456-1765-4 (pbk)

A CIP catalogue record for this book is available from the British Library and the Library of Congress.

Typeset in 10.5 on 12 pt Sabon
by Best-set Typesetter Ltd, Hong Kong
Printed in Great Britain by Hartnolls Ltd, Bodmin, Cornwall

This book is printed on acid-free paper.

CONTENTS

ACKNOWLEDGEMENTS

A first sketch of some of the arguments in this book appeared as 'L'impatto politico delle technologie informatiche: partecipazione o autoritarismo' in *Teoria Politica*, 5 (1989), pp. 95–110, following a conference organized by the journal and the *Quaderni del Circolo Rosselli* in Florence, 12 December 1986, as part of the city's celebrations of its cultural year of Europe. I wish to thank Alfio Mastropaolo for his help and comments; also, at later stages in preparing the paper for publication, Geraint Parry and Onora O'Neill. Benjamin Barber gave most generously of his time and attention in preparing detailed comments incorporated into a chapter which appeared in *Prospects for Democracy: North, South, East and West* published in 1993 by Polity and edited by David Held. The latter provided perceptive editorial comments as well as commissioning this book.

On the book itself, I have benefited a great deal from the judicious observations of my colleague Albert Weale, always with time to unravel a knotty point, and a detailed commentary from Michael Nentwich. Iain McLean's stimulating and provocative opinions on democracy have always been interesting to read and argue with. With such distinguished help I ought to have avoided making too many errors, but any which remain are most certainly mine, without a doubt! I only hope I can claim a share in the book's merits. These, if they exist, owe much to the help I have received from these colleagues, and from the invaluable research into direct voting conducted by (among others) Austin Ranney, David Butler, Pier Vincenzo Uleri, Mario Caciagli, Wolf Linder, Hanspeter Kriesi, David B. Magleby, Thomas E. Cronin and James Fishkin. They are all cited in the text and bibliography but without their ground-breaking efforts this would be a more impoverished discussion. All books which marry empirical research to normative evaluations of democracy draw inspiration from Robert Dahl's pioneering work, which it is only fitting to acknowledge in the dedication.

I. B.

INTRODUCTION

Challenges of Direct Democracy

The *traditional* challenge of direct democracy is to the limited participation of citizens in their own government. Why should responsible adults be debarred from deciding policies for themselves, on public as on private matters? Democracy justifies itself as empowering citizens, making government their own rather than an external or imposed authority. So it is hard to defend restrictions on democratic citizens' power to decide what governments should do and how they should operate.

The *new* challenge of direct democracy lies in the startling fact that it is now technically possible. Public policy can be discussed and voted upon by everyone linked in an interactive communications net. Such nets are spreading through the world, so they can easily carry debates among the citizens of any one State. This destroys the killer argument habitually used to knock direct democracy on the head, that it is just not practical in modern mass societies to bring citizens together to discuss public policy. The existence of electronic communications means that physical proximity is no longer required. Mass discussion can be carried on interactively even when individuals are widely separated. Hence opponents of popular participation need to find other, more cogent arguments, if they want to reject direct democracy as a way of running a country.

What we do in this book is to review these arguments at a serious level of detail; whether they are for or against direct democracy, and whether they are moral, theoretical or factual. Many modern developments seem to be pushing us towards direct democracy. The breakdown of traditional bonds and lines of authority, in society and the economy as well as in politics, has led to increasing demands for consultation and widespread protest when popular consent is not sought by governments. Governments themselves consult and seek to persuade much more than they did fifty years ago, when they simply ordered citizens to do things. They are encouraged in this by the post-war development of opinion-polling, which cruelly tests their claims to have popular support for what they do. The young and even the not-so-young are better educated than they were and more inclined to take (often effective) direct action when their passions are aroused. Press and television are more probing, and through them a greater consciousness of the personal impact of public policies has been diffused at every level.

All these trends have enhanced the influence of public opinion in contemporary representative democracies. It is not fanciful therefore to see these as eventually evolving into institutions where citizens publicly debate every important issue, and where there is formal as well as informal provision for popular voting on policy questions. Indeed some existing democracies, notably Switzerland, Italy and certain American States, already allow for this through their provisions for popular initiatives and recalls. We shall be looking in chapter 4 at how well such arrangements work.

Direct democracy, involving popular voting on all the important decisions now made in parliaments, is the most advanced form these tendencies could take. The fact that it does not exist at present is not to say that it could not emerge as a result of current developments.

Even if existing democracies go only some way along this road, it is still worthwhile to ask if they *should*. Are there good theoretical reasons why no country so far has adopted direct democracy (as distinct from the natural but selfish reluctance of existing power holders to share their privileges with others)?

Many respected writers, with no personal axe to grind, have expressed doubts about unlimited popular participation. Their arguments have to be given due consideration. At the very least their criticisms indicate the need for safeguards – institutional modifications and checks – which an uncritical advocate of 'people power' might wish to see swept away as unjustified constraints on the popular will.

As we will see, however, it is very difficult to stop arguments against direct democracy developing into arguments against democracy itself, including modern representative democracies. For if one argues that ordinary people are too ill-informed, unstable or fickle to be entrusted directly with making important decisions, the question immediately arises: 'Why should they be allowed to choose governments to make these decisions for them?' Surely politicians seeking election will play on popular ignorance or passions so that only the worst will get elected? Would it not be better in that case to find some other way than elections of choosing the government?

Various strategies have been tried to get round the problem of arguing against direct democracy without arguing against democracy itself. Possibly the most persuasive is to advocate mixed institutions which could balance popular representativeness with political expertise. The classic case for this kind of balance was made by the framers of the US Constitution, but the argument has been repeated with many variations since.

A major novelty of this book is to take into account another crucial invention of the last hundred years, the political party. This is not usually considered in theoretical discussions of democracy. But in fact it has a central influence on the way popular discussion develops and on the way voting is organized, under representative democracy just as much as under direct democracy.

Given the omnipresence of parties and their influence over every aspect of political life, one could maintain that the really crucial differences lie between countries with, and countries without, freely operating parties, rather than between different institutional arrangements which incorporate them. If this is indeed the case, many of the contrasts traditionally drawn between direct democracy and representative democracy may be irrelevant, as they ignore the really important characteristic of modern democracy, the pervasive presence and influence of parties.

All these points, together with actual evidence on the nature of participation and on the working of approximations to direct democracy, are taken up later in the book. We start by considering the moral case for mass participation and how far it is feasible given modern developments in communication (chapter 1).

The second chapter considers what kind of institutional set-up would be required to make mass decision-making possible. Direct democracy is often discussed as though its only possible embodiment would be a continuous mass meeting of citizens (or its electronic equivalent). But this is far from the case. One of the surprises which emerge once we take the possibility of direct democracy seriously is the sheer number of institutional forms it could take on. Many of

these meet traditional fears about a popular majority exercising unlimited and possibly tyrannical power, and worries about citizens'
capacity for unlimited debate and discussion.

Following this comparison of institutional forms, chapter 3 reviews
arguments against direct democracy and the ways they might be
answered.

We may seem in this case and in some following chapters to devote
too much time to defending direct democracy against criticism rather
than justifying it on its positive merits. The case for direct democracy
is strong precisely because citizen participation in decision-making
and the active consent of as many people as possible to public policy
are key democratic values, for the reasons we shall investigate in
chapter 1. We can thus assume their inherent validity and desirability
in a democratic context. Their beneficial effects have already been
eloquently urged elsewhere (for example by Pateman, 1970; Barber,
1984).

Opponents of direct democracy do not deny its moral appeal.
Instead they emphasize the undesirable consequences and inherent
problems of mass participation which unfortunately make its full
realization impossible or threatening. What we do here is to widen
the debate by suggesting a whole range of institutional forms under
which citizens might debate and decide policy. We then show that
some of them at least can withstand the standard criticisms.

Having reviewed theoretical arguments along these lines in chapter
3, we go on in chapter 4 to examine how mass participation actually
operates where it is encouraged. The nearest approach to direct
democracy in the modern world is where legislative votes are supplemented by referendums or popular initiatives on particular issues,
supported by a right of recall of legislation or of elected officials.
Initiatives have been of major political importance in Italy, but more
scope is allowed them in various American States. Switzerland is the
country where popular initiatives are allowed such weight that it is
closest of all existing democracies to direct forms. We shall examine
these cases with particular attention to see if the negative consequences predicted by critics do in fact emerge – particularly whether
party and government cohesion suffer as a result of popular voting
(chapter 4).

Having reviewed what actual evidence we have on the workings of
direct voting systems, we are in a position in chapter 5 to review some
of the arguments for and against direct democracy on a factual rather
than on a purely speculative base. *Are* political parties mortally

weakened under conditions resembling those of direct democracy? How do ordinary citizens react to making policy? Are the various criticisms about their incompetence, apathy, lack of time etc. borne out by the evidence?

In chapter 6 we draw on other factual evidence, this time about the nature of political debate. Quite a lot of the arguments about the desirability or not of extended citizen participation base themselves on a certain idea of how political discussion proceeds – that it involves sharply opposed alternatives, for example, so that decision-making usually pits a (temporarily) satisfied majority against a defeated minority. Much recent research indicates instead that discussion is about the relative priority to be given to a number of desirable actions, so that there is substantial agreement and chances for compromise between majority and minority positions. The tendency to separate out one policy area from another and to decide on each singly and individually also helps avoid some of the problems of collective decision-making which Riker (1982) and McLean (1989), among others, see as weakening the arguments for direct democracy.

The concluding chapter 7 considers not just the desirability of direct democracy from a moral point of view, but whether there is not a real need for more direct democracy to overcome some of the most pressing problems of modern politics. We can argue this above all in terms of the popular involvement and support so necessary to a healthy democracy – and more than that, to a functioning community. These have been discounted and devalued in the post-war period (cf. Berelson et al., 1954, ch. 14). However, they remain essential. A reliance on elites to keep things going in the face of apathy and withdrawal by the population calls into question how long a polity can remain democratic, if not its very right to call itself a functioning democracy. This, of course, brings the arguments of this book full circle, to the case now summarized in chapter 1 for both the desirability and feasibility of mass participation in decision-making.

1

Mass Participation and its Feasibility

1.1 Democracy and Participation

The evident failure of Fascist, military and Communist regimes to overcome their immediate problems, let alone achieve the millennium, has by the end of the twentieth century left democracy as the almost unchallenged alternative. Democracy has an irresistible allure for populations whose freedoms have been restricted and aspirations subordinated to some distant goal prescribed by regime ideology. Among other benefits, democracy offers citizens the freedom to choose for themselves – both privately, in deciding how they will lead their own lives, and publicly, through their participation in the collective choice of governments and policies.

The mechanism which democracies have for registering collective choices are regular, free, competitive elections, mostly involving a selection between parties competing for seats in the legislature, which will enable them to form or participate in government. As part of their efforts to appeal to electors, each party will put forward a general programme for action, and sometimes the election will also involve a choice between specific policies or will be supplemented by inter-election referendums, which also involve such choices at an even more specific level.

Elections are felt both to embody and to guarantee the main values which democracy promotes, which in turn are all linked to its claim to be the political system most sensitive and responsive to popular needs and aspirations. Citizens are regarded as the best judges of their own requirements. Voting for the party and the programme which best reflect these is seen as the most efficient way of registering and expressing them. Parties or governments ignoring, by accident or design, popular judgements about what is generally needed will be defeated in electoral contests, while those offering what the population wants will gain support, and with it the power to make decisions.

There are all sorts of qualifications to be made about these assumptions which we will consider later – such as what happens to minorities whose preferences differ from those of the majority. For the moment, however, we want only to examine the essentials of democratic arrangements in order to develop our argument about participation, and will consider later, in chapter 6, important qualifications about minority preferences (to which direct democracy may, however, provide some answers).

Put in the way we have stated it above, the argument for democracy seems essentially an interest-based one. Democracy allows the public to judge its own interests freely and to express what it wants, better than any other political arrangement. Elections and other democratic processes are designed to reflect and respond to the public's definition of its own interests and certainly not to impose predetermined goals upon it. If existing parties, tied to particular ideological programmes, fail to reflect popular preferences, new parties are free to challenge them and get support.

There are really two arguments bound up with the popular ability to express interests under democracy. One is the idea that the right to vote, and to form groups which seek votes, is the most effective way to promote interests and to safeguard them from being trodden on. Another strand is, however, the idea that interests are best *discovered* through free discussion in a democracy. Underlying this is the notion that interests are most efficiently identified by individuals themselves and that on the whole a person's interests are what (s)he wants and desires. The idea that a person's 'real' 'basic' interests can be specified from outside, independently of expressed preferences, is distrusted because it so easily leads to the authoritarian imposition of other people's preferences and interests on the person concerned. This also applies to common or collective interests arising from the need to regulate individual modes of choice and to deal with the unforeseen consequences of interacting individual decisions. The definition of these is also best performed by as many of the public as can collectively do so (Weale, forthcoming, ch. 3).

The way democracies deal with the possibility that people may be mistaken about their true individual or collective interest is to allow for more discussion, comment and if necessary argument. If in the end, however, a person or group remains unconvinced by counter-arguments and appeals to other interests, the tendency is to accept their preferences as valid ones.

Seen in this light the various democratic freedoms – of speech, association and voting – find their main justification in allowing for the safeguarding and identification of interests. They permit citizens to protect themselves against their individual and collective interests being ignored; they allow decision-makers to identify popular interests through these preferences which are expressed, and to check whether they are stable through their resistance to change in the midst of discussion and debate.

Freedom is also, however, often regarded as a value in its own right, not just as a guarantee for the pursuit and expression of interests. In this guise it appears as a condition for moral growth and self-development, independently of the interests it may serve or express. Making as many choices for oneself as possible improves the quality of choices that will be made in the future and one's self-knowledge and maturity.

To some extent these contrasting justifications find their roots in two great philosophical traditions of the modern world. Arguments for democracy in terms of its sensitivity and responsiveness to expressed interests are very congenial to the Utilitarian tradition, which takes what people want as the basic starting point for its philosophical and political systems. Arguments for democracy in terms of freedom as an absolute value go back on the other hand through Kant to Jean Jacques Rousseau and *The Social Contract* (1762/1973).

There are potential differences and divergences between the two positions. Indeed, Rousseau has often been criticized as overriding both individual interests and personal autonomy in the name of collective freedom. Critics have pertinently asked what kind of collective freedom it is which 'forces people to be free', thus doing away with the individual's right to choose. Liberals like J. S. Mill have also been seen as elevating freedom to a value separate from and higher than the individual's expressed interests and preferences, which may deprive it of many of the substantive benefits we prize it for (Lindsay, 1910, p. xv).

Since these writers laud the merits of citizen activism (Rousseau, of course, more dramatically than Mill), it might be felt that the ideal of mass participation falls under some of the same criticisms from the Utilitarian side as have been made of Rousseau's and Mill's general philosophical position. And indeed there is a tendency in Utilitarianism, best exemplified in the earlier works of its founder, Jeremy Bentham, and in the career of his disciple, the authoritarian social reformer Edwin Chadwick, to assume that the balance of particular interests leading to the Greatest Happiness of the Greatest Number is best known to independent legislators and bureaucrats who can simply impose it on the mass public without consulting them.

Following Bentham in later life as interpreted by the elder Mill (James Mill, 1823), the Utilitarian argument has, however, evolved into the position – well exemplified in contemporary economics – that the individual's expressed preferences are the only legitimate indicator of his or her interests. This supports the argument for democracy that we have made above. If each person is the best and ultimately sole judge of his/her best interests, and the object of public policy is as far as possible to advance these, this makes a strong case in the absence of other considerations for every citizen to participate in the making of public choices. For no one else will be in as good a position to express his/her interests, or to see how public decisions might affect them, as the individuals subject to them.

Given the extent to which Utilitarianism has been incorporated into economics, this argument for popular participation and choice is more often articulated for the market-place than for politics. There it often takes the form of the proposition that economic decision-making should so far as possible be freed from State control, so as to allow consumers – the best judges of their own interests – to make as many unconstrained individual choices as possible.

However, the argument for consumer sovereignty based on individual awareness of one's own needs can also extend very easily to the State, whatever sphere of action the latter controls. If what the administration does affects the citizen (as it is bound to do) then surely the latter, as the best representative and interpreter of the individual and collective interests involved, should be put in a position to decide what it ought to do.

In this way the argument from interests comes round to the conclusion, reached more directly by the argument for freedom as a goal in itself, that the greatest possible allowance for individual and collective choice, politically as well as in other spheres of life, is not simply a good thing but probably the most basic political value. As such its pursuit should be elevated above other, lesser goods such as stability, order and prosperity – though part of the Utilitarian argument is of course that maximal freedom is the best way to attain these goals too. This is because freedom, and the need for uncoerced consent to policies which it entails, does provide the best long-term basis for public stability and order on the one hand, while on the other securing the integration of the individual into society in a way which should contribute to prosperity too.

These goals will be achieved because the opportunity to choose improves the awareness of, and the ability to judge, one's own or one's group's interests (from the Utilitarian point of view) and contributes to moral autonomy and refinement of judgement from a Rousseauesque standpoint. A third strand in the argument for as much participatory democracy as we can get is thus its educational and self-improving value. We should desire more opportunities for making our own choices, both individually and collectively, because we become better persons by doing so. This could be expressed in practical terms of widening our sympathies with other groups and with society as a whole, as we have to consider these in the course of making collective choices. Deciding also increases our substantive knowledge through the debate, research and argument to which we are exposed in the course of making up our minds. This builds up our capacity to weigh up arguments and balance interests, and helps increase both our moral sensitivity and our potential for practical judgement.

Clearly these benefits come whether or not our views prevail in the final collective decision. To some extent therefore arguments for the educative and improving effects of political participation, as well as those based on the ultimate value of individual freedom as a good in itself, are immune from the criticism that could be made of interest-based arguments for popular choice. That is, what good does the ability to choose do if your interest is defeated – if you are in the minority on a decision?

You could still reply of course that in the long run your interests will be better identified and safeguarded in a democracy, through free discussion and extended freedom of choice, than under any other system. However, this argument is not convincing if you belong to a permanent minority distinguished by some indelible social characteristic, which faces the prospect of being permanently defeated on issues important to it. What use is clear identification of interests if the only result is for them to be slighted?

We shall return to this point in chapter 6. Its power is such that it does somewhat discredit interest-based arguments at this point, however. To be able to argue for the possibility of minority group members actually supporting a system which produces a balance of negative decisions from their point of view, one has to appeal to more idealistic reasons – to possibilities of self-improvement through making choices, and of having one's consent at least asked for.

However, one can also see possible difficulties in the argument for choice based on self-improvement. Suppose choices are made cursorily or evaded? Suppose – as many critics have argued – popular debate obfuscates rather than enlightens, and encourages decisions to be made in ignorance rather than knowledge? Would the case for greater participation then disappear? *If* such criticisms were true, we could still argue for participatory democracy, but not on grounds of self-improvement nor of its educative effects. We would have to defend it on some such basis as the need for free, unforced majority consent to what is being done in the people's name, and argue for this on the grounds that only consent can create a moral obligation to uphold the government and its policies.

It is perhaps for this reason that Beetham (1993, p. 61) maintains that the sole ultimate ground on which democracy can be justified is in terms of its respect for individual autonomy, which requires that the individual be asked to consent in some way to what is done in his/her name and to what will affect him or her.

However, this position again runs into difficulties with minorities who have voted against a collective decision. Unless democratic decisions are to be taken unanimously, not everybody's consent can be obtained nor their total autonomy guaranteed. In this strong sense, individual autonomy requires anarchy (where everyone has a veto on a collective choice) rather than democracy (Weale, forthcoming, ch. 4) – though surely it would also support the maximum possible debate and participation in the attempt to get unanimity.

We do not, however, need to commit ourselves to the full autonomy argument to justify the need for participation. All we need do is recognize maximal individual and group autonomy as essential to defining interests in a democratic context. If we do so, the interest-based and educative arguments will then take us most of the way along the road to justifying it. They do so because, when combined with plausible factual assumptions about the nature of democracy and of its citizenry, they are in fact quite resistant to the counter-arguments cited above. For example, if we affirm that in actual practice popular debate has a positive rather than negative effect on participants, we can save the educative argument for participation. And if we examine more closely the nature of the alternatives up for political choice and see where this leaves minorities, we can maintain that they need not be totally disadvantaged. Both points will be argued in detail later. If accepted, however, they leave the other justifications for participation with considerable overall validity.

In any case we do not for our purposes here have to choose finally between arguments which all point in the same direction – towards the need for as much participatory democracy as we can get. All the justifications sketched above are used to a greater or lesser extent in supporting the participatory case – and indeed, more generally, in arguing for democracy as such whether in its representative or direct forms. It is to the arguments for deciding between these forms that we now turn.

What must be emphasized before we begin this discussion, and at various points within it, however, is that representation does not negate the need for popular consent and participation. As against more authoritarian regimes, indeed, proponents of representative democracy make the case for participation as strongly as it has been expressed here. Only, in confronting direct democracy, they argue that it must be limited to the choice of alternative government teams and general programmes. Participation should not extend to the endorsement of particular policies, because of the practical difficulties that widespread and continuous participation would entail.

To appreciate these points more fully we need at this point to consider in more detail what is involved in democratic participation. This we do immediately, before going on in section 1.3 to consider what critics cite as the greatest practical difficulty of all – the very feasibility of having more popular debate and decision-making than we already have within modern mass societies.

1.2 Mass Participation and the Division of Political Labour

The word participation is often bandied about in discussions like this one as though everyone understood what it means. Like a lot of other political terms, however, it is often used in different ways by different people. A lot of disputes about 'participatory democracy' are caused by definitional misunderstandings of this kind, so a first need in this discussion is to clarify how we will use the term here.

Afterwards we will consider the types and frequency of citizen participation in existing representative democracies, before discussing how these must change, in both kind and extent, under direct democracy. This brings in the question of whether there are inherent barriers to participation deriving from the limits on the time and energy people have to spend on it. Emphasizing these limits leads rapidly to the concept of a division of political labour, where citizens limit their activity largely to voting and representatives make detailed decisions for them. This is often seen as the most rational (or indeed the only possible) way to organize a democracy – which must therefore be a representative democracy.

As this is a very common argument against the possibility of direct democracy, it is as well to face up to it immediately, before going on to arguments on the practical feasibility of mass discussion and voting, reviewed in section 1.3. First, however, we must define what we mean by democratic political participation.

A standard definition is 'taking part in the processes of formulation, passage and implementation of public policies' (Parry, Moyser and Day, 1992, p. 16). This omits some kinds of interaction with public authorities (filling in tax forms or visiting an office to claim welfare benefits, for example). Most people engaged in debate over the nature of democracy could probably agree with this exclusion, whether they were on the participatory or representative side. A more serious restriction is that the definition omits activity directed at informing oneself about public affairs – research into books or statistics, reading newspapers, listening or watching news and current affairs programmes or even discussing these with family or friends (Parry, Moyser and Day, 1992, p. 40). While one can act or react to public policies without informing oneself in this way, the quality of what one does is likely to be greatly enhanced by it, so much so that at least one analysis of political obligation (Parekh, 1993) defines political 'attentiveness' as a major duty for the citizen.

As the quality of citizen intervention in politics is one of the major points at issue between participatory theorists and their critics, it is in the extent to which citizens do and can inform themselves that one is likely to discover discrepancies in the use of the term participation. (See, for example, the emphasis on 'rich talk' in Barber, 1984). Clearly, if participation includes looking at TV news and current affairs, which almost everyone does, its extent and potential are much greater than if it is confined to overt acts aimed at changing or sustaining policies, especially when under existing representative set-ups these may be difficult and laborious to undertake.

With regard to overt political acts of participation, evidence about their incidence across major Western democracies is fairly clear-cut. The majority of the adult population votes in national elections – in most democracies 75–85 per cent do. Voting in occasional referendums on specific policies of major importance may reach this level but falls off if there are many such votes. Turnout in regional and local elections is lower – 30–70 per cent across Western Europe and North America.

Outside voting, acts with political significance are rarer and generally undertaken by a smaller proportion of the population. The most recent national study of participation (in Britain but with results quite typical of other national studies) discovered that almost 8 per cent of the adult population had attended party meetings; about 14 per cent took part in informal group and 11 per cent in organized group activity related to politics; 21 per cent had contacted a local councillor. On the other hand 63 per cent had signed a petition on some political matter and almost 15 per cent had attended a meeting to protest against some policy (Parry, Moyser and Day, 1992, p. 44).

This is not unimpressive. However, there are two qualifications on the findings. One is that most people do not act in these ways very often: on average British adults had engaged in only four of these kinds of action in the previous five years – three of which might be voting at the different levels of election (local, national and European). Another was that people tend to specialize in different areas: someone who did party work, for example, is unlikely to attend protest meetings and vice versa (Parry, Moyser and Day, 1992, pp. 47–62, 253). 'Gladiators' engaged in all arenas of politics are rare.

The limited extent of overt action outside voting, coupled with what has been taken as widespread popular ignorance and naiveté about politics (Berelson, Lazarsfeld and McPhee, 1954, ch. 14) has supported an argument that this is all that democratic populations are capable of. To summarize this argument, which crops up repeatedly in the following chapters. It is clear, for the reasons given in section 1.1, that the population needs to be consulted in general terms about what government is to be formed and what general line of policy is to be pursued by it. Their own lack of interest and lack of information about politics makes it necessary to confine their role to the essentially passive one of voting for competing leadership terms at widely spaced general elections. To seek to involve them any more – for example on a regular basis in deciding specific policies – is simply unrealistic. At best it will hamper governments and decision-makers who ought, because they are better informed, to be left free to pursue specific policies within the general programme they have put forward. At worst it will lead to demagogues playing on popular ignorance and passivity to pass policy proposals on low votes manipulated by their supporters. In the end this might lead to the overthrow of democracy itself. Far better therefore to stick with the limited opportunities which representative democracy offers for participation, which gives popular opinion as much of a say as it is capable of having – and even the possibility, for those more active and involved than the average, of influencing decision-makers in other ways, as evidenced by the findings above.

Participatory theorists want more than this. While they welcome any extension of opportunities to discuss and influence public policies, the main thrust of their argument is towards more direct popular involvement in deciding specific policies. This is for two reasons:

1 Election of a government team at intervals of three, five or even seven years does not give the public much influence over the policies pursued. These may change for either internal or external reasons and the government can thus institute quite different priorities from those it was elected on. Coalition governments in particular may change, so even the leadership team differs from the one that was elected. Such non-elected governments may take cues from public opinion or be subject to pressure from petitions or demonstrations, but the popular majority are quite unable to enforce their preferences on such non-elected bodies.

2 Even where an elected government serves its full term on the programme it was elected on, there is a question of whether choosing between two general policy packages does not blunt the force of majority preferences on specific policies. Taking a quite typical case, British electors may be invited to choose between two party packages, in a representative election, one of which emphasizes the importance of defence, lower taxes and traditional morality while the other supports the welfare state and closer regulation of private industry. On balance an elector may choose to support one or the other. In doing so, however, (s)he may well have to suppress concerns about welfare in order to promote concerns about morality and security. Why should (s)he? As there is no logical or necessary link between the various policies parties put together as their programme at elections (Budge, Robertson and Hearl, 1987), public opinion would surely be better reflected if electors were free to vote on the separate policies as they come up, rather than being constrained to a once only, overall choice of a general package every five years. (For a more formal development of this point see chapter 6 below.)

Better opportunities to meet with and influence representatives are all very well therefore. However, reforms in this direction – which could be accommodated within the existing representative framework – still leave the balance between populace and representative heavily biased in favour of the latter. (S)he is not constrained to follow popular views and – being beholden to special interests, bound to a particular ideology, and concerned to advance a political career – has in many cases little incentive to do so.

However much participatory theorists may welcome better access to representatives or a relaxation of State controls on popular expressions of opinion (which are generally quite extensive), the nub of their case rests on making more public policy directly subject to popular enactment, rather than this being left to governments and Parliaments as it is under representative democracy.

Given this position, they can counter the argument about the need for representation based on a presumption of popular apathy, by pointing out that when it comes to voting – the key act of political participation in a democracy – the overwhelming majority turn out to do so. High turnout occurs not only in representative elections but in many direct votes on public policy where these are permitted. Not only do electors vote in large numbers on specific questions put to them by governments and Parliaments (referendums); they are also capable, where this is allowed them, of organizing petitions to have issues put to a popular ballot. They turn out in high numbers to vote on such initiatives. (See chapters 4 and 5 below for detail.) Even where less than 50 per cent of an electorate vote on policy matters this still opens the matter to decision by infinitely more than if the decision were taken by (at most) 600 or 700 representatives. If we seriously pursue the arguments in section 1.1 about individuals being the best judges of their own and the collective interest as it impinges on themselves, any extension of participation must be a good thing. Hence, institutional arrangements should be changed so as to encourage it. This means, as we shall see, that representative democracy ought to be broadened out into direct democracy by allowing for direct voting on specific issues.

As far as the findings on current levels of participation are concerned, this argument emphasizes that the empirical evidence by no means points one way, to the prevalence of popular apathy and inertia. It is a question of seeing the bottle as half-empty or half-full. From a participatory point of view the extraordinary thing is that popular voting, which in representative elections has only a tenuous connection with the governmental policies subsequently pursued, maintains itself at such high levels. The fact that as much as a quarter of the population then goes on to further political activities, often of a largely symbolic character owing to the indifference or active hostility of entrenched governments towards them, is quite extraordinary. It attests more to popular involvement and interest than to apathy.

The argument about allowing electors only occasional involvement in representative elections is from this point of view both hypocritical and self-fulfilling, in that it actively discourages popular political involvement both in theory and in practice. Any other kind of political action than voting has major barriers set against it in representative democracies, precisely because pro-representation arguments make it suspect and vaguely illegitimate, because it puts pressure on representatives who have been elected for the very purpose of deciding policies independently of electors.

At the very least therefore we can conclude that the evidence on actual popular participation and involvement in democratic politics does not 'objectively' favour the representative argument. It can be interpreted two ways, and there is at least a case for saying that it demonstrates a potential on the part of ordinary electors for more active involvement, particularly for voting on policies, than is currently allowed them.

There is, however, a reinforcing argument which can be, and is, commonly deployed against the participatory position. Though theoretical in nature, it builds on the previous evidence, interpreted again as demonstrating a limited capacity on the part of electors for political involvement. Limited involvement, it is argued, is entirely rational, as can be shown by the analogy with the economic division of labour.

As Adam Smith pointed out long ago, a product can be made much more efficiently by dividing up the tasks associated with its manufacture, with each worker or section of the workforce performing only one operation. Economic specialization of course goes much further than this, to the level of the whole macro-economy. Thus some specialists organize production while others distribute the produce; others again provide finance and buildings or services. It would make no sense if consumers, for example, tried to do all this for themselves. They would simply take time from other activities they enjoyed, while products would be fewer and worse in quality than what they could buy through distributive chains from mass manufacture. Everyone is better off therefore if supply and distribution are left to entrepreneurs to organize while the consumer buys their products and organizes the rest of his or her life as (s)he wants to.

Applying this argument to politics involves accepting that ordinary citizens cannot do everything for themselves. In politics too there are entrepreneurs – the politicians – who deal in policies as economic entrepreneurs deal in products and services. Rather than citizens trying to invent policies for themselves, which requires inordinate research, great inventiveness, and much effort in debating and implementing them, it makes sense to specialize. Most people just do not want to make the commitment of time and energy which these political tasks would entail. They have much more interesting and pleasurable pursuits – family, sport, culture, media, hobbies – from which politics would take inevitably limited time. Thus it makes sense to leave politics mostly to the politicians, just as in economics the provision of necessities is left to entrepreneurs. The profit they extract from their activities can in both cases be regarded as legitimate payment for their efforts (Dahl, 1970, pp. 40–60; Sartori, 1965, p. 254).

The argument against extended popular involvement in politics can be further reinforced by the likelihood that once one group of people started to put forward policies, others would be forced in defence of their own interests and preferences to participate more too. In turn other groups would become involved to defend their own position, and so on. Such 'defensive' participation could extend indefinitely, dragging reluctant and hostile groups into interminable discussion and confrontation until exhaustion set in. This would lead either to the victory of the group with most stamina or to shortcutting the process by violence, which would bring an end to democracy. Better far then to stick to the division of political labour embodied in representative democracy where detailed discussion and formulation of policy is left to the people who make a career of doing so. They may have defects but are able to settle on policies within a finite time and without the inordinate costs which would be incurred if every person became his/her own politician.

From a participatory point of view the objection about 'defensive participation' is of course not necessarily a wholly negative feature. If we are to believe the argument in section 1.1 (commonly used by defenders of representative as well as of direct democracy), active involvement in discussion and debate is a good thing as only in that way can interests be defined and defended. More of such involvement is to be welcomed, up to a point.

The nub of the criticism, however, is that there is no point where it can stop. Each group will drag the others in however unwillingly, and the resulting stand-off will be prolonged indefinitely in the absence of rules for a closure.

But this of course begs the point. Why in a participatory system would there *not* be rules for a closure? The argument certainly applies to unstructured mass meetings where there are no rules for debate, and rambling unfocused discussion goes on forever, rather like student meetings in the late 1960s during the tide of protests and revolts that shook Western universities at that time. But there is no logical or practical reason why a direct democracy should always take this form. Even in one which depended on mass meetings there could be rules of debate. And in ones which (more realistically under modern conditions) depend on popular debates conducted through the media, and on postal voting, there is no way debate could continue indefinitely. In Switzerland, which among modern democracies approximates most closely to this form of direct democracy, there is clearly a certain defensive mobilization of groups against each other in popular votes. But discussion and voting are conducted quite expeditiously and lead to clear-cut results without imposing intolerable costs from participation. Such would be the case in any feasible form of modern direct democracy.

There is in all these arguments a premise that political participation is for most people a disagreeable diversion from other more agreeable pursuits. Clearly, while some may enjoy canvassing and organizing, many of the acts of political participation identified by Parry and his co-authors (1992) are laborious and may well be disagreeable. Voting, signing petitions and attending meetings, however, are such widespread practices that they may be more enjoyable or at least less costly than is supposed and they of course are at the centre of the proposals for extending participation through popular discussion and voting on specific policy proposals.

If we extended the definition of participation to actively informing oneself and being attentive to politics, as participatory theorists would urge, the distinction between agreeable private pursuits with benefits and disagreeable political ones with costs would, however, almost totally disappear. The television and radio programmes most generally and spontaneously followed are the news (21 per cent of total viewing time in Britain in 1990). Documentaries and features take up 8 per cent of viewing time, closely trailing sport at 11 per cent. Even light entertainment (17 per cent) comes below the news in popularity, which is rivalled only by drama (surely not devoid of political content) at 24 per cent (HMSO, 1992, p. 178).

The point is that the tired executive or worker switching on TV to relax in the evening is just as likely to turn on the news or current affairs as to watch anything else. Television and radio have largely abolished the distinction between leisure and information, entertainment and politics. The abolition may have other consequences, not all positive, but it certainly undermines the cost argument. Voting through some electronic device in each home, as described in the following section, would also be easy and follow naturally from relatively costless home viewing and discussion.

This new consideration goes some way to undermine the division of labour argument. If there are no costs and indeed some pleasures in the major relevant forms of participation, there is less reason to delegate the activity.

The major criticism of the idea of a division of political labour enshrined in representative democracy must be, however, that it is based on a false analogy with economics. Consumers *do* benefit from firms undertaking manufacture and distribution for them, but they do not delegate them to choose on their behalf at the supermarket shelves. That would be the equivalent in economics to representatives choosing for them politically between public policies. To delegate in this way is to run the risk of many interests remaining undefined and ignored because of lack of general involvement – just as consumers having choices made for them would be only crudely if at all satisfied economically (as the Soviet Five Year Plans demonstrate).

Of course, had a population to engage in all the processes of policy formulation and research currently undertaken by politicians and specialists, heavy costs would indeed be incurred and the objection from the division of labour would be upheld. As we shall see, however, there are perfectly viable forms of direct democracy where specialists and politicians formulate and propose policies and bureaucrats implement them. The difference from current representative forms is that the population votes directly on the specific policies they come up with, not just on general policy packages or competing government teams.

This situation provides a more exact analogy with the economic division of labour than representative democracy does and avoids the major costs of doing everything oneself equally efficiently. Just as economic consumers cannot delegate their choices without undermining the rationale for the market, so electors cannot delegate their political choices without undermining the rationale for democracy.

Electors in most discussions of democracy where economic analogies are used are conceived as consumers (cf. Downs, 1957). So this refutation is quite convincing. Some proponents of the argument from the division of labour might try to save it, however, by arguing that citizens are more properly regarded as *producers* of the collective goods which are constituted by public policies. The analogy therefore is with the factory or the firm. Surely, it is argued, one would not propose that all the workforce should make all the decisions for the firm. The question of whether to go in for a new product, or indeed how to organize production overall, should surely be left to directors or managers and not be decided by mass meetings or votes.

However, this extension of the economic analogy cuts both ways and does not wholly support representative democracy either. Like many arguments used against direct democracy it actually has wider and more radical implications and tells against democracy as such rather than against one form of it. For of course directors and managers are not elected in most economic enterprises and are certainly not representative of the workforce (nor, in most cases, are they really representative of shareholders: they are self-perpetuating). Pushed to its extreme therefore the idea that the State is like a business, with a hierarchy of subdivided functions, and decisions made at the top, would argue against having any kind of democratic decision-making at all and in favour of some kind of authoritarian hierarchical structure. This would not be what proponents of representative democracy want but it is the implication of relying on a vague analogy with the productive division of labour.

One problem with the analogy indeed, like many other arguments reviewed below, is that it is generally introduced into the discussion as though it was perfectly clear what it involves and constituted an unchallengeable point in favour of representative democracy. When examined in detail it then turns out to have many ambiguities and not necessarily to support the representative case at all.

Thus it is by no means clear that general decisions about launching a new product or entering a new market or seeking new capital are entirely technical and best left to management. Technical factors of course enter in but cannot be determining – for example, they cannot guarantee that the product will sell or that there will not be difficulties in production (which the ordinary worker may be better aware of than directors or managers). So it is by no means clear that decisions will not be improved by general debate or even mass voting within the firm.

Practical evidence on this comes from the relative success of firms in post-war markets. It is generally accepted that over this period the most successful enterprises have been German and Japanese ones – particularly in comparison with companies in the English-speaking world. A major difference, which has often been regarded as one of the reasons for German and Japanese success, lies in the degree of influence allowed to the workforce and shareholders. In both cases the banks, the major shareholders, are consulted continuously on the development of the firm by its managers. In contrast Anglo-American directors are notoriously independent of shareholders and the only constraint on them is the fluctuation in the price of their shares in financial markets. These usually react to the last set of profits produced by the company leading to the 'short-termism' (lack of concern with long-term development and investment) widely believed to have been responsible for a decline in British manufacturing.

In contrast, consultation and collaboration with shareholders in the German and Japanese cases has led to a willingness to ride out short-term crises which would bankrupt British factories and to plan ten or twenty years into the future. This has maximized profits in the long run and enabled companies to dominate world markets in their sector.

With regard to the workforce it could hardly be argued that Japanese firms were models of democracy: like Japanese society as a whole they are organized on distinctly hierarchical lines. Nevertheless they are notable for the way they seek to involve and actively consult workers on all matters affecting production processes. German firms go much further towards industrial democracy. Their Works Councils have a right to be consulted on development and investment plans and they have powers of decision on social and personal matters. Contrast these practices with the average British or American firm whose major interest is in reducing labour costs and retaining maximum managerial control to hire and fire.

While these powers are often defended as necessary to business survival, which type of firm has been more successful? The answer is plain to see – those firms which have encouraged shareholder and worker participation. While they are far from economic democracies, the evidence would seem to point to more participation and involvement in the firm as a condition of success.

Thus economic analogies even on the producer side do not provide an unequivocal argument in favour of restricting popular participation in democracies. The clearest examples of business democracies are co-operatives. There have been spectacular cases of the collapse of co-operative production enterprises (usually ones set up as a political palliative to run failing factories). However, individual organizations like the Co-operative Wholesale Society in Britain, Mondragon in Spain, dairy co-operatives in Ireland and wine co-operatives in France and Italy have all functioned well over a long time. In the retail and services sector such organizations have been spectacularly successful.

Why then has industrial democracy not become the norm? The answer lies not in any inherent logic of the economic division of labour (though greater participation may well give a competitive edge to some firms, as we have seen). Rather it involves our beliefs about the extent to which the individuals and groups affected by collective decisions should have a share in making them. In other words, the economic argument at this point merges into the general political one. Many businesses, especially multinationals, are bigger than small States and affect their members' lives as much. The arguments for turning them into democracies, and whether these should be representative or direct in form, are just as relevant as for any other politico-economic association (cf. Dahl, 1985) and are discussed below in that context (chapter 6).

The economic analogy with the division of labour breaks down at this point because it depends on the same political premises as we are discussing anyway. Enough has been said about its other aspects, whether they invite us to see citizens as consumers or producers, to indicate that it does not favour representative over direct democracy – not unless the latter is identified with the proposition that the citizen should combine all the tasks of parties, politicians, bureaucrats, interest groups and media. But that has never been urged even by such extreme theorists as Rousseau, let alone appeared in the workings of any of the direct democracies we know about. Even ancient Athens had primitive political parties, specialist politicians and persons delegated to administration (Bonner, 1967, pp. 23–4, 45, 61–2). The economic division of labour only works as an argument against greater popular involvement in decision-making if the latter is caricatured. Unfortunately, we shall see that setting up a straw man and then demolishing it is a widespread form of argument in this field, though I hope it will be discredited by this book.

1.3 The Feasibility of Mass Debate and Decision-making in Modern Democracies

General discussions about the relative merits of representation and popular participation tend to have a rather abstract and make-believe quality. That is because of the difficulty, however hard we try, of envisaging a whole national population organizing itself sufficiently to discuss policy and decide on political alternatives. Even if we make an allowance for politicians and political parties working in this setting, widespread participation often seems a Utopian ideal rather than a practical possibility.

The purpose of this section, however, is to argue that modern technology has made it easy to have frequent popular votes with supporting discussion. It also gives a first sketch of how they could be organized. This will be fleshed out in chapter 4 by seeing in practice how popular policy-voting works in countries where it already exists like Switzerland and the United States (at sub-national level).

The importance of showing that direct mass involvement in policy-making is feasible derives from the fact that democracy in all its forms bases its claims on its unique sensitivity to popular opinion, through its encouragement of open debate and voting. In justifying democracy against its opponents therefore we are bound to stress the dependence of governments on popular approval, through regular elections and other mechanisms, and the importance this gives to popular discussion and to widespread participation in democratic political processes.

The fact that democracy as such is both defined and defended through its encouragement of participation, and dependence on consent, gives the theoretical case for direct democracy an irresistible initial boost. Direct democracy, as we shall see in more detail, is about opening up political processes to the whole of the population, by letting citizens vote directly on matters currently reserved to Parliaments. If, then, popular participation is such a good thing, how can one possibly oppose any extension to it and still remain a democrat?

This is a crucial question which will reverberate throughout our discussion. It puts opponents of direct democracy on slippery ground. Indeed, in criticizing extended popular participation they often do slide over into generally anti-democratic arguments (as we have already seen) rather than ones exclusively focused on direct democracy. This is one of the commonest counter-criticisms which can be used in favour of direct democracy, as will appear time and time again in the following discussion.

To square the circle of criticizing direct democracy for its advocacy of extended participation, without criticizing democracy for advocating participation as such, opponents often fall back on practical objections. One is the argument from costs to a division of political labour, which we have just reviewed. Another is to claim that mass debate is not 'proper' or 'real' debate, because it does not allow for a presentation of balanced arguments (chapter 3).

By far the most popular 'practical' objection, however, relates to the very feasibility of mass debate and voting. For practically the whole of the modern period, indeed, the possibility of direct democracy has been raised in theoretical discussion, usually in regard to the idealized democracy of Athens, only to have it pointed out that the size of modern States renders a face-to-face meeting of citizens impossible. This holds whether the States in question have half a million or 200 million inhabitants. In neither case could the citizens physically assemble together to debate policy. Without the possibility of face-to-face discussion, debate is impossible and must be delegated to Parliament. J. S. Mill in *Representative Government* (1910, pp. 217–18) typifies this form of argument. The possibility of direct democracy at national level is raised and dismissed with this reasoning in three sentences.

It is worth looking briefly at the functioning of ancient democracy to see how it compares with modern alternatives. The city-state of Athens between 450 and 350 BC is the best-known example. The city and surrounding territory had an estimated 80,000 inhabitants. Only adult male Athenian citizens participated in the popular Assembly, however, excluding children, slaves, foreigners and women. Within these severe limits the potential membership was probably of the order of 20,000–30,000, but actual attendance much less, at most 6,000 – even though citizens were paid to attend (Bonner, 1967, pp. 47, 108).

In terms of real size therefore the Athenian Assembly was probably not much larger than some constituent assemblies of our own day. Its powers, however, were total. Not only did it legislate on all policy, it also decided on its implementation down to the least important details. The officials who carried through its commands were chosen for limited periods and by lot, so that they lacked any authority or power base in relation to the Assembly. Individuals like Pericles who wielded great influence did so by their continuing ability to carry the

Assembly with them through their eloquence – and, importantly, through building up a political organization not unlike a modern political party (Bonner, 1967, pp. 45, 61).

Debate and decision-making carried on in this manner were very time-consuming. A large part of the adult citizens' time was expected to be spent in Assembly and in political discussion. This ideal of almost total immersion in public projects has exerted a considerable attraction for theorists since, and the arguments we have reviewed on the educational effects of participation and on its moral worth were first rehearsed by Greek thinkers.

Clearly the Greek model is unworkable today and functioned badly in Athens too, much of the time. It is hardly a means for extended participation either, given the exclusion of the vast majority of the population from debate and voting. Yet discussions of democracy have assumed that a mass popular meeting of this type is the only form that direct popular decision-making on policy can take. Clearly it is impractical in any society outside the Ancient Greek, so if we accept that it is the sole possible embodiment of direct democracy we must rule that out as a viable alternative for the world today.

Even in the nineteenth century, however, this argument from impossibility was specious. Even though the Greek model was imperfect, there were other possibilities. The press offered a means of general information (and through letters and comment, of debate) which had simply not existed in Greek times. The Post Office and other government bodies could rapidly diffuse and collect letters and pamphlets, as well as voting forms. These provided the technical basis, still in use today, for popular referendums and other types of political decision-making such as the initiation of legislation or recall of officials (chapter 4 below).

It is true that a political debate carried on through the printed word is slow and incomplete. Many – perhaps most – are excluded from discussion through lack of education or access. Nevertheless enough are reached and involved to characterize debate as genuinely popular – certainly in comparison with both the Greek Assemblies and modern Parliaments.

Overlooking these possibilities and concentrating on the Greek Assembly as the only possible form for direct democracy seems in this context less of an oversight and more of a rhetorical tactic to evade serious discussion on the relative merits of democratic systems. The representative form was presented as the only possible way modern democracy could function as such – which it clearly was not.

When the possibilities of print were supplemented by telephone and radio, then television, this was even less true. The phone-in, the televised debate, the casting of mass votes after debate, all opened up discussion to strata of the population which would never have got a look-in at Athens. (For an investigation of popular debate based on phone-calls and broadcasts see Hollander, 1985; Arterton, 1987. Their analyses put beyond doubt the feasibility of popular debate and voting by those means, even before the most modern technical developments like video conferences became a possibility.)

It seems then that the means for extending popular participation in decision-making, if not for having a fully fledged direct democracy, have been in place for a long time and ignored rather than seriously considered as a basis for democratic decision-making. If doubts remain about the capacity of these channels to carry full-scale popular discussion comparable with debate in parliament, they should, however, be dispelled by the technical developments of the last thirty years. These involve above all the computer and the facilities for communicating with it and through it.

It is hardly necessary to stress for readers who will mostly have a computer of their own, and be linked into an interactive network, the communicative potential of computers (they are eloquently sketched in McLean, 1989, pp. 61–107). As computer users cannot fail to be aware, new developments extend their communicative potential all the time. The most pertinent for our argument is the union of computers with telephone and television and the likely presence of such a combined device in almost every household in the early years of the next millennium.

Such a combined device would receive vocal instructions from its owner, transmit and receive words and images, and have the same unlimited linkages with others as telephones have now. It only needs the universal distribution of devices (by the State if necessary), and the organization of this network by some kind of central committee or moderator, for it to transmit a political discussion in which all those nominated by the organizer(s) could speak. The techniques for organizing such discussions are already well known from television and radio chat-shows and video conferences. Only official approval and possibly a secretariat similar to those which now serve legislatures are necessary to give this kind of electronic discussion an authoritative voice in making political decisions. If this were done it would institutionalize direct democracy in a modern form.

Clearly the technical and social basis for direct popular discussion and decision-making among millions of citizens is already here. There may be practical limits on how far everybody who wished to speak could (as in modern parliaments – unless the debate were to be indefinitely protracted – there would be limits of time). By sampling and other methods of selection, a moderator could make sure that all points of view were heard. This does of course give power to the moderator but again no more than to the president of a legislative chamber and (s)he could be bound by the same norms and entrenched procedures. All this goes to show that:

1   The argument against the practical feasibility of direct democracy is totally invalid, probably for the past, certainly for today. Direct popular participation in debate and voting is rendered not just possible but easy by the electronic media, which also reduce if not eliminate the costs associated with it. These electronic media are still supplemented by the print technology which has facilitated mass participation through referendums and initiatives in the past.

2   Debate can also be fully interactive. Direct democracy based on electronic communication need not be 'the citizenry sitting before a video and allegedly self-governing itself by responding to the issues in the air by pressing a button' (Sartori, 1987, p. 246). Interaction can be two-way. Full mass participation must be constrained by time, and individual interventions will depend as always on personal psychology and skills, particularly on speaking and presentational skills. In any conceivable scenario a moderator would have to select participants.

To the question 'who would moderate the moderator?' the answer must be that such an official would operate under the same legal and role constraints as legislative officials do now. In this sense mass debate is not inherently more subject to manipulation than legislatures are today.

1.4 The Quality of Electronic Debate

Even though the more obvious forms of distortion could be taken care of by rules and roles, there is a more subtle critique to be made of electronic debate. Is interaction at a distance through machines – necessarily depersonalized to some extent – really the same thing as face-to-face discussion in the same room? Talking over a political problem in company and at length, in a physically congregated assembly, is clearly a different experience from contributing to discussion with unknown interlocutors.

Clearly this cannot be denied. The experiences are different. Face-to-face discussion may well produce greater understanding of other people's position, more constructive suggestions, nudgings towards compromise, reluctance to push matters to an extreme, and even willingness to delay a decision so participants can mull over it. Not all of these characteristics result directly from actual physical proximity of course, but from the relative absence of time constraints and the more relaxed attitudes that go with it. However, physical presence will permit a greater response to non-verbal stimuli, for example, than electronic interaction, no matter how sensitive the transmitters and receptors are.

These features of small physical meetings are ones very much valued by participatory theorists such as Pateman (1970) and Barber (1984, pp. 117–34). Barber indeed regards them as important features of 'Strong' Democracy. Not only does this form of participation have greater educative effects for the individual, it also strengthens the social and personal links without which democracy becomes simply a set of purely formal procedures. In turn social ties strengthen willingness to compromise and strengthen the ability to offer alternatives on policies such as 'decide in six months' time after further discussions'. In short, face-to-face contact produces 'rich talk' rather than formal debate (Barber, 1984, p. 367), which is a highly desirable outcome.

However, from a broader view, not all the benefits are on the side of physical contact or the costs on the side of electronic debate. Barber's vision of mass participation has been criticized – a point made earlier by Dahl (1970, pp. 40–56) – for the enormous amount of time and energy it would consume, which most people might well be unwilling or unable to contribute. The long, leisurely, rambling discussion necessary to produce compromise and agreement within a neighbourhood might not be to everyone's taste. Indeed, it is possible to see it producing frustration and anger, which could spill over at the meeting into dramatic confrontations and community conflicts – which are just as much features of small-town meetings as consensus.

The very impersonality and large-scale nature of electronic debate might avoid some of these personal costs, as well as being more economical in terms of time. But is it so fundamentally different from face-to-face debate that it can only be contrasted with it rather than similarities found? It is a moot point, for example, whether a change from personal to a telephone conversation does make a radical difference to discussion. Would such a transfer produce as marked an effect as a switch in the natural language in which the conversation was conducted, for example? This has a considerable potential for altering the import of political words and the level of abstraction of the discussion.

The general point surely is that any change in the venue of discussion (Sartori, 1987, p. 284), in the numbers involved, in the media or language through which it is conducted, or in the interlocutors present or contactable has a potential for affecting the terms of any debate. At the extreme therefore one could insist that no decision-making not conducted in Greek in a popular assembly of classical type could be termed direct democracy.

Surely, though, popular debate and discussion, however conducted, have certain characteristics in common which make them recognizably the same. A telephone conversation differs from face-to-face conversation but both are recognizably conversations. Similarly one might claim that an electronically based debate – provided (an essential point) that it permitted interaction and dialogue – allowed for decisions to be made on broadly the same lines as in actual popular assemblies which themselves now rely heavily on electronic devices like microphones, internal television and voting buttons. (This is the broad conclusion reached by Hollander (1985) and Arterton (1987) on the basis of their own research and extensive reviews of findings in the field.) Both electronic and face-to-face debates can be regarded therefore as variants of direct democracy – a point which reinforces the one made in the next chapter, that direct democracy may take various institutional forms, which need to be specified before we can consider detailed arguments for and against them.

Moreover, contrasting electronic with face-to-face debate as if they were incompatible alternatives is misleading. Having one by no means rules out the other, as the dependence of legislatures on these systems indicates. Barber points out (1984, pp. 281–311) that all his suggestions for stimulating participation could easily be carried through while preserving all the institutions and competences of representative democracy as we have them today. Similarly, face-to-face discussion could coexist with electronic debate and even be stimulated by it.

One could well imagine for example that owing to constraints of time in the national debate, local groups could be formed by interested parties to hammer out a common position and nominate a spokesperson to intervene in the general discussion. Another channel for small-group participation would be for official agencies to pick a representative sample which could either straightforwardly debate the decision under discussion or publicly go through the kind of seminar with experts suggested by Fishkin (1993), expressing opinions and taking votes as they went along, in a preliminary and advisory mode. Multiplied on a regional and local basis, such groups could be important channels for precisely the informal and moderating discussion Barber has in mind.

If face-to-face discussion and electronic debate are viewed as complementary and even as mutually reinforcing, there is little point in asking whether one is inferior to the other in a general way. Conceivably we could combine the strengths of both. It is also likely that having more popular debate and decision-making at one level would stimulate it at the other.

The more relevant question is, perhaps, which is the level at which more popular involvement is likely to be stimulated first? There is an argument that electronic debate, because of the lesser costs and smaller demands it imposes on individual citizens, could be implemented nationally in the foreseeable future. The rest of our discussion will therefore base itself on this mode of decision-making, with the reasonable expectation that encouragement of more face-to-face participation would be one of its results.

The quality of debate is only one worry expressed about electronic networks in a democratic context. Two others rapidly emerge in any discussion. The first is the possibility of central monopoly and control, which instead of allowing the populace to influence government would enable government to control the populace. This danger is of course present in representative democracies just as much as in direct democracies (Margolis and Mauser, 1989), particularly in regard to television. It needs to be averted by adherence to ground rules guaranteeing independence and general access – which, as will be argued below, could be present in direct just as much as in representative democracy. The tendency in electronics has in any case been towards interactive networks in which the audience ceases to be the passive recipient of messages and itself contributes to them. Progress in the field has produced a growing diversity of sources and channels, both in mainstream computing, linked by telephone, and in broadcasting (citizens' band radio being an example). We are much further from the vision of a Garrison State (Lasswell, 1941) based on huge central computers and a communications monopoly than we were earlier in the post-war period.

The second fear is that direct access through electronic media would enable demagogues and potential dictators to appeal to the alienated and anomized masses with dire consequences for democracy (Kornhauser, 1960). Again, however, where this has happened it has been under representative forms, so it seems no *more* likely to happen in direct democracy. Indeed the greater sophistication and involvement that participation, even in electronic debate and decision-making, might give to the population could even act as an effective barrier against demagogic appeals (Barber, 1984, p. 160). Moreover, if the argument made in chapter 2 about parties operating under direct democracy is accepted, these would form the same barriers to demagogues as they do under representative democracy.

The case of the 1992 Perot candidacy for President of the United States (in a representative democracy!) is instructive. Once exposed to the full cut and thrust of electronic debate, his appeal rapidly eroded among the population at large. At the beginning, his candidacy seemed a textbook case of the power that can be obtained through demagogic use of the media. In the end, however, the media seem to have crippled the demagogue – simply by giving ordinary citizens grounds for making a better-informed judgement on him. If anything, Perot gives us good grounds for trusting popular exposure and good sense rather than excluding population and media from decision-making.

Nor can the meteoric rise of Silvio Berlusconi in the 1994 Italian general election be used as an argument to demonstrate the inherent demagogic effects of television which would be intensified in an electronically based direct democracy. The crucial point about Berlusconi's rapid build-up of a personal vote was that representative democracy in Italy had failed abysmally to regulate the political coverage of television in any fair way (or any way at all), or to rule against concentration of media ownership. As a result Berlusconi was able to make outrageously biased use of the half of the national network which he owned while claiming equal shares on the rest. It was, however, the failure of regulation, necessary in both representative and direct democracy, which accounted for his success, not the inherent defects of televisual coverage itself. Indeed a comparison of Perot's failure and Berlusconi's success is instructive in what it tells us about the need for effective media regulation in all forms of democracy.

The case for regulation to ensure balanced debate is argued in more detail below. What we can say here is that in themselves electronic networks, especially as they are likely to develop, are neutral between various political possibilities, but they do create a physical potential for direct mass debate and decision-making which has not existed since the evolution of modern states. The technical feasibility of this clears the way for reconsideration of the theoretical arguments and factual evidence about the way direct democracy would work, which have a practical relevance now that they never had before.

1.5 The Need for a Serious Assessment of Direct Democracy

What this chapter has done is to clear some of the undergrowth from the debate on direct democracy, which enables us to see both wood and trees more clearly. Most discussion of the subject is inadequate because it has been blindly focused on only one point. Advocates of direct democracy have urged the case for full popular participation in decision-making as the only really democratic way to obtain consent to policies, ignoring any other difficulties extended participation might cause. Opponents have evaded the basically unanswerable point about democracy requiring participation, by emphasizing the practical impossibility of arriving at decisions through popular debate and discussion and making incorrect analogies with the economic division of labour. When they have gone on to make other objections these have on the whole been ill-considered and superficial, in two respects. In the first place they have been directed at a parody of a system of popular decision-making, in which an apathetic, badly informed population is manipulated by special interests to vote on issues in a chaotic and shifting way: pressing buttons and calling it democracy, in Sartori's phrase. Little attention has been given to how citizens actually behave when they *are* consulted (see chapter 4 below).

Critics have thus concerned themselves with only one of the possible institutional forms of direct democracy, where popular discussion is totally unstructured and uninformed by experts, parties or procedures. When this has been shown unsatisfactory, as it easily can be, they have concluded that they have destroyed the whole case for direct democracy, without reflecting on how the arguments about representation would look if we took a chaotic parliamentary system like that of the French Fourth Republic as the form all representative democracy must take.

Proponents of participation on the other hand have tended to feel that once the moral case for it was made – and it is, probably, unanswerable – this was all they had to do. But in a multi-valued world where stability, order and justice might be argued to be the first concerns of the State, the effects of unlimited participation on these and other values have to be weighed up. This is what critics of direct democracy have done when they have ventured beyond their opening feasibility gambit. And they have a point. If participation, however valuable in itself, has negative effects on other values, then it may need to be limited to secure a balance of benefits. Whether this is in fact the case we shall see in the following chapters.

2

What are Direct and Representative Democracy?

2.1 A General Definition of Direct Democracy

So far we have been talking about direct democracy without specifying exactly what we mean, though a general impression has probably emerged from discussion. If we now attempt to pin this down, we can characterize direct democracy in the abstract as a regime in which the adult citizens as a whole debate and vote on the most important political decisions, and where their vote determines the action to be taken. Whether the body of citizens then oversees implementation of their decisions, as in Athens, or leaves administration to an accountable government or bureaucracy, seems immaterial at this level of discussion. What is important is that the policy or action the majority have voted for is carried through.

Applying this very abstract definition to the circumstances of contemporary democracies, we can translate it into the operational requirement that the body of adult citizens discusses and votes authoritatively on most of the matters on which, in representative systems, parliament now debates and votes. It could be objected that parliamentary approval is in most countries a rubber stamp for decisions made by governments. Party leaders, who form the government, are able through internal discipline to get their followers in parliament to vote as they want.

Whether one thinks it a good or a bad thing, there is no doubt but that this is a substantially accurate characterization of the way most representative democracies operate. Popular voting, even if it extends over the same areas as parliamentary, is bound to be less tightly constrained by party ties, however. So approval could never be taken entirely for granted, as in some existing legislatures. This does not mean that popular voting would necessarily be chaotic or incoherent either, though some would criticize it as likely to be so because of lessened party control. Again this is a point which we need to investigate on the basis of actual evidence, which we do below (chapter 4).

It should be made clear also that substituting popular voting on the most important decisions does not necessarily mean that parliaments need be abolished. They could be retained in a variety of roles. One would be as a committee to debate and set the wording of the policy alternatives to be voted on by citizens. Another would be to stage an advisory debate or even an advisory vote on the matter under discussion. Still another would be to oversee detailed administration of policies endorsed by the population – a task parliaments are supposed to perform now but which they rarely have time or resources to do properly, given the complexity and autonomy of modern administration.

What should be clear from this is the fact that the essential feature of direct democracy – citizens taking the important decisions – is compatible with many types of institutional arrangements, including existing representational ones. The sole requirement by which we can judge whether direct democracy exists or not is the involvement of all adult citizens in directly debating and authoritatively deciding all the most important policy questions. Below, we review some of the differing forms which direct democracy could take. Some of them have obvious flaws and some much less so. What is important is to remember that they are all direct democracies.

2.2 The Classical Conception:
Unmediated Rule by the People

Representative democracies differ greatly in their institutional forms and types of government – from two-party systems with single-party majority government, to multi-party systems with coalitions, under parliamentary systems; and on to the separation of powers and election of the Executive in a Presidential system. Nobody would deny, however, that these are all representative democracies. It is typical of the cavalier theoretical treatment direct democracy has received that it has generally been associated only with one variant – unmediated direct voting – with no other possibilities being taken into account or even with them being explicitly ruled out (Bogdanor, 1991, p. 177).

There are, however, other obvious variants, against which it is much harder to muster objections than against the unmediated form.

Here we contrast unmediated popular voting with a highly mediated system, though there are clearly many other half-way houses between them.

The classical conception of direct democracy is of a system of unmediated popular voting. All political decisions are put to popular discussion and vote, so the executive has more or less of a routine administrative role. There would be no political parties, no advisory bodies and no entrenched rights: propositions would be put to the sovereign people for immediate decision after popular debate, transmitted through the electronic media discussed above. All political decision-making thus approximates the referendum campaigns in systems with substantial powers of popular initiative and recall. Politics would be a perpetual referendum, where the sovereign people were urged to vote for or against a variety of issues, technical and otherwise, ranging from ecology to nuclear war, budgetary provisions to education, morality to penology. There would be no constraints on these expressions of popular will – not even from their own past decisions – since a current majority could always overturn a past one.

Despite considerable evidence for popular restraint and good sense under situations approximating to this (cf. Cronin's comprehensive review of American State initiatives and referendums, 1989, pp. 231–2), it is easy to see how such a set-up could confirm the worst fears of critics and opponents of direct democracy. Decisions would often be inconsistent with each other and ill-considered. One alternative could be carried on a great wave of emotion at one point, only to be partially abrogated or contradicted in another measure months later – or abrogated altogether once the implications become clearer. Budgetary constraints would not be considered, partly because proposals are voted on separately. So everything tends to be regarded as desirable and attainable, rather than any realistic rank-ordering of expensive policies being made. (For a review of these features of American State experience see Magleby, 1984.)

These problems might be compounded, moreover, by interventions being covertly promoted and indeed initiated by interest groups, whose machinations might only be revealed too late. Referendums sometimes stimulate a temporary influx of ill-informed and normally apathetic electors whose participation adds further unpredictability to the result and introduces greater inconsistency and incoherence to the process of decision-making. An additional fear is that popular majorities would not limit themselves, so that minorities would be disregarded and even suppressed before they had the opportunity of transforming themselves into future majorities (Sartori, 1987, pp. 115–20).

On the positive side, supporters of the system can argue that actual experience with referendums does not support these fears (Cronin, 1989, *passim*) and that it is in any case unrealistic simply to extrapolate from such referendums to full-blown direct democracy. However influential present-day referendums may be, they exist essentially at the fringes of representative systems. Participation is sporadic and occasional precisely because of the sporadic and limited nature of the referendums themselves. It is thus unable to serve the educational purposes it would do in a fully participatory democracy. Popular ignorance and irresponsibility follows from limited participation. Advocates of direct democracy argue for the self-improving and educative effects of debate and decision-making (Pateman, 1970, pp. 1–20; Barber, 1984, p. 152), which might in the long run lead to majorities themselves imposing limits on their actions.

Whether the educational influence of participation would counteract the defects listed above is, however, debatable. Limits on the energy and time even of an informed electorate would leave them open to manipulation by interest groups and demagogues. Some institutional safeguards are needed which would approximate arrangements in current representative democracies with some referendums, which is not far from what we already have in Switzerland and California. So why change?

In making a fair assessment of the claims of direct democracy it is vitally important to realize that some of its other forms are capable of providing for institutional safeguards which meet many of the criticisms sketched above. Unmediated voting of the kind just described is usually focused upon by opponents as though it were the only possible institutional embodiment of direct democracy. But there are in fact many other ways it could be institutionalized, starting with the party-based direct democracy we examine next.

2.3 A Mediated Form:
Direct Democracy as Party Democracy

It is easy to understand why both proponents and critics of direct democracy instinctively identify it with the unmediated system described above. If the impulse towards direct participation is impatience with institutions which prevent the popular will from directly expressing itself, the natural response is to sweep them all away as impediments to popular sovereignty (Rousseau, 1762/1973, pp. 260, 269–74, 369).

However, direct democracy can also be seen as a pragmatic way of adapting essentially nineteenth-century institutions to the vast social changes – above all in education and communication – which have taken place in the last sixty years. From this perspective there is no need to sweep away existing institutions which are functioning adequately, or which might be redefined so as to fit usefully into a new framework. The same is true for constitutions and legal safeguards (free media access, for example) which limit or slow down the impact of political decisions. All are as compatible with doctrines of ultimate popular sovereignty as they are with doctrines of ultimate parliamentary sovereignty in most democracies today.

This consideration could apply to parliaments functioning as advisory bodies, as suggested above. But above all it could also apply to political parties, which have taken over the role of mediation between populace and government (Sartori, 1987, p. 148). Although this is recognized in passing in discussions of direct and representative democracy, most comparisons between the two systems usually ignore parties, implicitly assuming that they would be absent in direct democracy and somehow do not affect the relevant aspects of representative democracy. Yet parties are the great political invention of the last two centuries, without which representative democracy could not function at all in the modern world. Parties are the only bodies to review, reasonably systematically, developments and prospects for the whole society, and to propose a medium-term plan for dealing with them. They are also the only political bodies with enough cohesion and organization to carry their proposals through in government. They focus elections round their own issues and candidates (Budge and Farlie, 1977, 1983) organize legislatures (Budge and Keman, 1990) and systematize relations among representatives themselves and between them and their constituents (Matthews, 1973, pp. 121–3; Jewell and Patterson, 1973, pp. 36, 209–12, 373; De Winter, 1992, pp. 386–93). The careers of professional politicians and of representatives are inextricably bound up with the parties (Mastropaolo, 1993, pp. 11–84). All this would be anathema to Madison (1787–8/1911, pp. 41–2 – see chapter 3 below) but it represents a necessary and constructive response to problems of policy consistency and co-ordination in a modern society.

Given this, it is practically inconceivable that, under modern conditions, a direct democracy could function without political parties. Indeed, one of the problems identified by Cronin with the generally non-partisan initiatives and policy referendums in the United States (1989, pp. 70, 83) is the lack of the information voters would get from party endorsements of one side or another on the issues they have to decide. Within the more pragmatic approach to direct democracy, there is of course no reason why parties should not function as policy-initiating and clarifying bodies as they do today under representative forms. Nor is there any good reason why parties should not adopt substantially the same role in guiding and organizing popular voting on policies as they do now for legislative voting.

Certainly parties could not function entirely in the same way in regard to the population-as-legislative-assembly as they do in regard to representative Parliaments. Their stance might well be midway between the one they now adopt at elections and the one they adopt inside the Assembly. One cannot argue that a change from representative democracy to direct democracy would be without its effects. However, this is far from saying that it would inevitably destroy parties.

It is certainly true that in the United States the rise of the mass media and particularly of television has been linked by some with 'the decline of American parties' (Wattenberg, 1990, pp. 105, 166–7). By this is generally meant an erosion of their electoral and organizational base and in the ability of party caucuses to select their own candidate (as opposed to having a primary election among party supporters). Looking at the other aspects of American parties, such as their near-monopoly supply of candidates for office at State or Federal level, their control over government, and ability to match the policy-priorities they have put forward in elections with national expenditures (Budge and Hofferbert, 1990), their decline does not seem self-evident. They have changed. They place less value on traditional labour-intensive methods of campaigning and hence on membership. They are more attuned now to popular demands through chat-shows, phone-ins and media commentary than they were. However, the failure of Perot (and other third candidates before him) to break into election competition without a supporting party clearly demonstrates their continuing power, both electorally and governmentally, under conditions of mass media exposure.

The American parties have always been looser as organizations than their equivalents in other parts of the world, though this can be exaggerated (Klingemann, Hofferbert, Budge et al., 1994, ch. 8). What we have said about their continuing ability to place themselves at the centre of decision-making thus applies even more forcibly in other countries. Parties have adapted to media exposure, with a consequent decline in membership which is no longer needed to mobilize the vote. But they continue to dominate electoral and legislative voting, control governments and carry through their preferred policies. They have extended their activities to local and regional government. They are clearly able to survive media exposure and indeed to thrive on it. There is just no evidence therefore that parties could not survive wider popular involvement in policy debate through the media. They would simply adapt further (though not necessarily along the same lines, as increased popular participation might also increase their need for members again). I shall document these points in chapters 4 and 5 on the basis of party experience with extended popular participation in Italy, Switzerland and the United States.

What this implies in terms of comparisons between direct and representative democracy is that, where both are dominated by parties, the sharpest contrasts between them will disappear. The same tasks of organizing the agenda and ensuring minimal policy coherence will be performed by parties – possibly with little change between a Parliamentary and a popular setting, as they have increasingly to perform in the latter anyway, under today's conditions. One can indeed envisage a type of direct democracy in which there is a party-based government, chosen by elections. This government would put important bills and other political decisions to popular votes, just as it does with legislative votes under representative democracy. To get these votes through it could utilize both official and party-based means of persuasion, again following present-day practice.

There is clearly a greater possibility of government measures being defeated by popular vote than by legislative voting with strong party discipline. This raises the possibility, at the extreme, of a totally disrupted and inconsistent programme being enacted in a party-based direct democracy. Within the institutional framework we are discussing there would be, however, a variety of ways to avoid this possibility, without foreclosing avenues for popular debate:

1 Measures already included in the ruling party(ies) programme at their election might require a qualified (e.g. two-thirds) majority against, to be rejected.

2 Any measure which the government chose to make a vote of confidence might require a qualified adverse majority to be rejected (perhaps only in its first two years, to ensure an adequate term).
3 Governments could be fixed-term or variable-term. In the latter case various entrenched measures such as 1 or 2 above could be adopted to ensure them a reasonable life.
4 Measures need not of course be passed by one vote. There could be first, second and third readings, as in contemporary legislatures. Votes themselves need not be yes or no except in urgent cases: they could include other alternatives, as suggested by Barber (1984, p. 284), such as yes/no with qualifications or 'leaving back for consideration in six months'.

All these variations are perfectly compatible with a system in which a popular vote substitutes for a parliamentary one. Parliamentary voting is far from unmediated and unconstrained, and popular voting might be institutionally constrained in precisely the same way without departing from direct democracy in a general sense.

Critics might well object that institutions cannot be expected to function in the same way as they do in the parliamentary setting: and in particular that political parties could not maintain their internal cohesion in the face of voting whose outcomes they could not ultimately control through the imposition of party discipline. As against this one can point to existing representative systems such as the American Presidency in its relations with Congress; or the Italian parliament, where party discipline in the representative assembly is weak and the possibility of adverse outcomes always present. The numerous minority governments within the representative systems of Continental Europe also face the possibility of defeat unless they can build voting coalitions, often on a measure-by-measure basis. Parties have different characteristics in these contexts as compared to those they assume under tightly focused, highly disciplined single-party governments. But they are still recognizably political parties. There is no reason therefore to anticipate that parties facing popular rather than legislative voting would lose their essential characteristics or their usefulness in focusing and mediating popular concerns. This is borne out when we see how parties operate in contexts with a lot of popular intervention (chapters 4 and 5 below).

Clearly there are many institutional 'mixes' between unmediated forms of direct democracy and highly institutionalized forms. (Barber, 1984, pp. 281–311, eloquently presents a detailed scheme for one of these.) However, what is clear is that if critics want to deliver a conclusive blow to the moral and practical arguments for direct democracy, they need to concentrate on the institutionalized form just described rather than the unmediated one. The former is highly resistant to the traditional arguments used against direct democracy while the latter has so many undesirable features that in spite of some abstract appeal it functions as a straw man, easily knocked down by practical objections.

2.4 Modern Representative Democracies: Are they so Different?

Looking at the alternative forms direct democracy could take helps caution us against sharply contrasting it with representative democracy as though there were no viable compromises between them. The temptation is to conduct discussion as an either/or dichotomy – *either* direct democracy *or* representative democracy. In fact, we really have a continuum with many intermediate positions between the extremes. This is illustrated in figure 2.1.

The continuum is constructed on the basis of the varying degrees to which popular majorities determine individual policies such as the environment, taxation, finance, defence and so on. The model for unmediated direct democracy, where popular majorities determine everything, is always taken as Ancient Athens about 400 BC, though adult male citizens were at most 40 per cent of the total population at that time. In practice, the Athenian Assembly probably generated something like a crude party system: such organization was the only way statesmen such as Pericles and Demosthenes could maintain continuity and control. Hence the actual democracy of Athens is shown as nearer the party-based direct democracy we have been describing.

This kind of mediated direct democracy, where popular majorities are guided by institutions such as political parties, and constrained by various entrenched procedural rules, is shown more towards the middle of the continuum, though on the direct democracy side (we have already stressed that such an institutionalized system is just as much a direct democracy, in its basic and essential aspects, as the totally unmediated form).

Defining the other end of the continuum is the 'ideal type' of representative democracy, where all policy decisions are made by the

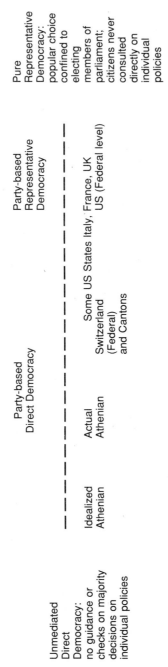

Unmediated
Direct
Democracy:
no guidance or
checks on majority
decisions on
individual policies

Idealized
Athenian

Actual
Athenian

Party-based
Direct Democracy

Switzerland
(Federal)
and Cantons

Some US States
US (Federal level)

Party-based
Representative
Democracy

Italy, France, UK

Pure
Representative
Democracy:
popular choice
confined to
electing
members of
parliament;
citizens never
consulted
directly on
individual
policies

Figure 2.1 A Direct–Representative continuum, showing intermediate or mixed systems between the pure types

representatives and the government they support and citizen debate and voting is limited to choosing representatives. Such a pure form of representative democracy does not exist in practice anywhere in the modern world, because of the activities of political parties. Even where the forms of representative democracy are maintained, citizens can choose between alternative programmes for government put forward by the parties. These enable them if they so desire to register an opinion on the general priorities which ought to guide the government though not on particular policies within this general package.

Even this limited electoral influence over policy suffices to move countries like the UK and US (at Federal level) a little way towards direct democracy. The ability to choose between policy packages at regular general and Presidential elections is supplemented moreover by the sensitivity of governments to movements of public opinion as registered by polls and published in newspapers. The UK and US are, however, placed only a little way over towards direct democracy because governments can and do ignore public opinion on specific points when it suits them to do so, and when general elections are far enough away for them not to be punished for it. The absence of formal mechanisms to make public opinion about what to do in specific policy areas really count politically serves to line them up near, though not at, the end of pure representation.

There are some representative democracies, however, which have quite extensive provision for referendums and other expressions of popular opinion. These are in some cases binding, and in others constitute authoritative expressions of opinion on very important issues. Thus Italy, not normally regarded as a country where popular opinion is much heeded, actually had several important questions such as divorce and abortion decided by referendums in the 1970s and had crucial constitutional changes put to the vote in the 1990s. Formally many of these referendums were simply advisory or abrogative of existing provisions but they put enormous pressure on governments to endorse the policy-line being supported. France is in a somewhat similar position given the President's ability to bypass the Assembly and put questions to a popular vote, particularly on foreign policy and constitutional matters.

Even further towards direct democracy are the Swiss cantons and American States, with extensive provisions for binding popular consultations on all sorts of matters. Switzerland as a whole also has these and we shall investigate how they work in practice in chapter 4.

These provisions make the difference between such systems and the party-based direct democracies envisaged in section 2.3 more a matter of degree than of principle. However, all these countries and States have powerful parliaments and governments with policies and authority quite independent of continuing popular endorsement during their term of office. Thus they are still nearer the representative end of the continuum. They do, however, offer the best indication of how direct democracy might work out in practice, given the relatively large role which initiatives and referendums play. So we shall look in chapter 4 at how popular debate and voting function in these systems, in order to check how far various assertions and counter-assertions about participation actually hold water when confronted with relevant evidence.

For the moment figure 2.1 illustrates how direct and representative democracy may actually merge into each other in practice. Sharp theoretical contrasts which prophesy disaster if democracies establish more direct procedures, or fail to do so, are therefore rather exaggerated, given the variety of actual practices which exist in the world today, and the absence of distinctions between them. (For example, the US veers towards being a pure representative democracy at Federal level and quite a long way towards direct democracy in constituent States.)

2.5 Representative Democracy and Constituency Relationships

Given the variety of practice among representative democracies themselves, it is as well at this stage, before reviewing the arguments for and against the two forms, to specify in more detail what we mean by representative democracy. As in the case of direct democracy, this will help us distinguish between arguments directed at straw men which do not really exist, rather than at the actual working forms. Looking at how modern systems work also casts more light on the role of political parties, which themselves are modern inventions not really dealt with in traditional arguments, but which do in fact help bring the functioning of direct and representative democracies closer together.

The essence of representative democracy, as the name implies, is the election by adult citizens of deputies or representatives who will then form a legislative assembly with the dual function of electing and controlling a government, and deciding on specific policies. A variant on this system, in Presidential systems, is that the head of the Executive is elected directly by citizens, and decides on specific policies jointly with the elected assembly. One reason for doing so is to build checks and balances into the representative system so that a President and parliament, with separate powers but needing each other's approval, can control each other (cf. section 3.3 below).

Representative democracy is often discussed, particularly in English-speaking countries, with prime reference to the relationship between legislators and their constituents. There are two major normative/descriptive models of this: Trusteeship and Delegacy.

The first conceives representatives as being selected for personal qualities, above all judgement, which in the opinion of the majority of their constituents render them best qualified to defend and advance the interests and needs of the constituency. Representatives are therefore selected as the best people for the job, not on the basis of issue-opinions. They then owe it to the constituency to use their best judgement in deciding how to vote in parliament on the issues that come up. They are not bound, in other words, to vote on issues as constituents think, if in their judgement another course of action is better. Constituents can judge their representatives' record at the next election and possibly reject them. But they cannot impose their views in between.

The Delegate model of relationships takes entirely the opposite tack. Legislators are elected to represent the views of constituents and should not oppose their personal opinions to the constituents'. If the conflict is too violent to be borne they should resign the position and let someone who is in agreement take over. On this theory delegates should continually consult constituents to keep up with their views on new issues, so that they can represent them effectively in the legislature.

There are one or two further variants on these ideas, such as the Guild Socialist contention that representatives should be the same as their constituents on all relevant social-economic characteristics, in order to facilitate an automatic transmission of their views. However, the Trustee and Delegate theories represent the leading alternatives (and indeed, the polar opposites) on the question of how constituents should be represented. The Delegate theory is interesting in the present context, as one might well ask whether a strictly mandated representative is not simply a roundabout way of implementing direct democracy. If representatives are simply to reflect constituents' views, could not direct popular voting do this better? (Unless the objective was to give special weight to the constituency, but if this were desired direct voting could be organized on a constituency basis.)

It is interesting therefore that the Delegate conception has been around as long as representative democracy itself, certainly from the beginning of the nineteenth century. It is sure to be invoked in one form or another by constituents whenever there is a difference of opinion with their representative – just as Trustee ideas will be invoked by the representative. The closeness of these conceptions to practical issues partly accounts for their longevity. But if the Delegate model is near the heart of conceptions of Representative Democracy, its close kinship with direct democracy forms another demonstration, if that is needed, that the two forms need not be that far apart.

Clearly, however, the implicit reference point in most contrasts and debates is a trusteeship version of representative democracy, because it is on the need for professionals and experts to make political judgements which ordinary citizens cannot make that much discussion about the superiority of one form to the other ultimately turns (Sartori, 1987, pp. 130ff). The trustee model is employed in tandem with the unmediated model of direct democracy to make a dramatic contrast. Such a contrast is effective rhetorically but hardly illuminating, given the nuances and wide range of diverse practices on the side both of representative and of direct democracy, which may effectively merge into each other. We shall return to this point when we review arguments on both sides (chapter 3).

The Trusteeship and Delegate models share the characteristic of being both moral and normative in character – specifying how relationships between the constituents and their representative ought to be conducted – and descriptive – saying how they are conducted in practice. Actual studies of the relationship in the United States (Miller and Stokes, 1963) and Britain (Budge, Brand, Margolis and Smith, 1972, pp. 80–123) have shown that no one model holds over all issue-areas. On Civil Rights, for example, American research showed that in the 1950s congressmen's opinions corresponded closely to the views of the majority of constituents (and where this was lacking they were less likely to get re-elected). On the other hand representatives went flatly against constituents' opinions on local taxation in Britain, even though a majority of electors felt fairly intensely about keeping it down.

Actual research into constituency relationships throws into relief factors ignored or taken for granted in theoretical discussions. These are above all constraints imposed by lack of information and of time and resources to remedy the lack. Putting things more directly, representatives often do not know what constituents' opinions are on most issues, and constituents are often ignorant of what their representative is doing on the vast bulk of matters which do not receive great publicity.

Ignorance and constraints on remedying it figure largely in the question of how well qualified citizens are to make their own decisions, as we shall see in chapter 3. The findings of these studies could actually be used on both sides of the argument. On the one hand, citizens are not well informed politically. But on the other hand neither are their representatives, despite the greater resources at their disposal. One simplifying device on both sides is adherence to political parties. French Deputies could make fairly accurate estimates of the (majority of their) constituents' opinions by simply attributing to them the party position on the issue, on the grounds that they must share it because they had voted the Deputy in (Pierce, 1992)!

2.6 Representation by Political Parties

Although much discussion of representation has focused on constituency relationships, it is important to bear in mind that many countries have representative democracy without constituencies. This is because of the need for systems of proportional representation (PR) to elect representatives within very large areas (up to the State itself in some cases) in order to ensure an exact translation of percentages of popular votes into percentages of Parliamentary seats. Here the concern has shifted from getting representation of a territorially defined group (the constituency) by an individual, to ensuring that the popular votes received by a party grouping of candidates match the proportion of seats it gets. Party in this case has taken over from constituency as the defining unit of representation. Its influence is strengthened by the fact that candidates run on a party list, whose composition is generally decided by the party leader rather than by local selection committees. Thus, not simply the election of a representative but his or her ability to run as a candidate at all depends on the party organization.

This influence of parties is not, however, confined simply to PR systems. It has clearly extended over to constituency-based representation as well – to such an extent as to blur any contrasts with non-constituency-based voting arrangements except at the margins. This is for two reasons. One is the decline of autonomous territorial communities through their integration into regional, national and international networks. This has been reflected in the increasing arbitrariness of constituency boundaries – now conceived as subject to considerations of purely numerical fairness and equality, rather than old ideas of representing 'natural' communities.

The other reason for the decline of constituencies, as anything other than a means of aggregating votes, is the rise of parties in the last 100–150 years as the predominant means of organizing democratic politics whether at electoral or governmental level – and indeed as the main way in which these two are linked. No longer can politics in representative democracies be seen as individual legislators deciding on matters, as either delegates or trustees, as they come up before them. They cannot even be seen as securing their own election through self-nomination and campaigning. Selection is strictly controlled by central organizations supervising local party committees, while campaigning is financed and organized by party officials. Except in exceptional cases candidates attract a mere 5 per cent or less of the constituency vote in their own right. The vast bulk comes on the basis of affiliation to a party.

What is attractive to electors both in constituencies and under PR is the party programme and record, and possibly its leader – information about which are transmitted to them directly by the media. The dependence of individual representatives on the party to get re-elected, and their commitment to the programme and general priorities which they have endorsed, ensure that the party will vote as a cohesive bloc in parliament.

Under these arrangements, which prevail in all modern democratic systems, representative democracy has become party democracy. The focus is on the relationship between the cohesive party and its supporters in all areas of the country. The mandate in question is the party mandate to carry through the policy priorities it has stressed in the course of the election campaign, not the representative's mandate, either to use his or her individual judgement or to forward the views of the constituency.

Given the centrality and predominance of party in these arrangements, it is a moot point how much difference would really be made by shifting votes on policy from parliament to populace. Debate has already spilled over through the continuous and unrelenting attention of the media to politics, and the fact that popular reactions to political developments constitute a staple of news. Provided – an important qualification – that parties continued to organize popular voting as they now do parliamentary, there might be relatively little difference between a direct party democracy and a representative party democracy. The mechanisms through which parties steered debate and guided voting would clearly differ, but the end result could be much the same. The party leaderships, indeed, might be more stimulated and revitalized by the challenge of winning a popular vote – where the outcome might always be in some doubt – than in trooping masses of obedient voting-fodder through the legislative lobbies, as they do in many countries today.

2.7 Other Intermediate Forms

The idea that representative and direct democracy do not sharply contrast, when both are operated by political parties, is reinforced by various suggestions that have been made for increasing the scope of popular consultation within a basically representative set-up. One way this has already been done in practice is by combining a representative (party-dominated) set-up at Federal level with extensive opportunities for popular consultation at regional or local level on issues pertaining to the sub-units. (However, since in the modern world most problems are shared, what one region decides on an issue like abortion has repercussions on others and effects at national level.) We shall examine how this territorial separation works in practice in chapter 4.

Another way of combining popular debate and decision-making with representative forms is by issue-area. Many modern democracies make provision for referendums to be held on important constitutional decisions, and, possibly, on a varying number of other fundamental points of policy. The recent Austrian, Swiss and Scandinavian referendums on entry to the European Union are examples. On the other hand, most of these countries, with the exception of Switzerland, restrict popular participation outside the constitutional area. This limitation on popular powers leaves these countries open to a variant of the objection aired in the first chapter. If 'the people' are qualified to take fundamental decisions about the whole context in which politics takes place, why are they not qualified to decide on other important substantive questions which may affect them even more directly? The question seems unanswerable unless other considerations are brought in, such as the limited capacity of citizens for extended political involvement. These will be considered in the next chapter.

When we move beyond actual decision-making to involvement in debates on specific policy – where citizens are brought in in an advisory capacity to inform representatives making the actual decision – the range of alternatives becomes even wider. The most influential and extensive mode of consultation is an advisory referendum, where the whole population votes after extensively broadcast and reported debate. Formally and procedurally, an advisory referendum is conducted like a full-scale referendum, the only difference being that the ultimate vote is not legally binding on the government. The political context, however, usually makes it very difficult to go against popular opinion, particularly when it is clear-cut and the government itself has initiated the consultation. (We shall examine the effects of these in Italy in chapter 4.)

Less extended but more continuous are Parliamentary Commissions on the Swedish model. All-party, charged with preparing legislation before particularly important bills or with reviews of policy in a given area, they are committed to the widest possible consultation before making recommendations to Parliament, where these usually form the basis for what is done. Such devices ensure that all Swedish parties have an unusually high influence over government policies (Klingemann, Hofferbert, Budge et al., 1994, pp. 155–71). They also ensure that all organized interests are consulted. This obviously gives ordinary citizens more of a chance to join the debate than in most existing democracies. However, when compared with referendums, phone-ins and letter-writing, an appearance before committees of enquiry represents a relatively high investment for individuals as compared to organized groups. Such groups themselves may be more or less responsive to their members, of course, and make more or less provision for rank-and-file debate before they take their official position.

The Swedish commissions represent the most influential and accessible form of committee hearing in modern Western democracies. All parliaments have committees of various kinds which give opportunities for extra-parliamentary and extra-governmental voices to be heard. The extent to which they can actually influence policy rather than just complain about it is variable but mostly restricted. And most are much less accessible than the Swedish ones, dealing mainly with recognized interests alone.

In examining the operation of modern representative democracies, it is necessary to go beyond formal procedures and even the role of political parties in assessing the degree of popular participation in policy-making. No account could be balanced which ignores the day-to-day attention paid to opinion polls on a variety of topics and the mass of discussion and interviews with affected persons carried by press, radio and television. Much more of this is published at a more specific level than ever before – itself a technological effect of improved methods of communication and of sampling and interviewing.

The impetus given by the democratic belief in consent means that once popular opinion on a question is known it is difficult to brush aside in deciding the matter. Thirty or forty years ago political argument could range over the question of what public opinion on an issue actually was. Now that a reasonably authoritative statement on this actually appears in print, it becomes an important asset in the case of one side or another in the argument. This is not to say that it automatically prevails, of course. As governments have authority to make the final decision, they can choose to ignore opinion, generally on the grounds that it is uninformed about the wider considerations involved in the decision or that the preferences expressed contradict ones expressed on related issues. These are arguments that we shall encounter in the next chapter. Suffice it to say here that representative governments do not generally feel it incumbent on themselves to see how the public might resolve the contradiction but instead use it as a reason for making their own decision.

Thus public opinion as currently expressed in representative democracies does not substitute for direct participation, though it is still fair to recognize its considerable informal role in representative debate. The other side of the coin, however, is that opinion does not simply influence governments – governments can also heavily manipulate public opinion (Margolis and Mauser, 1989) and the communications media. Even where the means stop short of direct corruption they may include biased appointments to State-controlled media, alliances with proprietors, specially commissioned polls to get an acceptable public opinion, massaging of official statistics and selective access for favourable journalists. All are ways to secure favourable media comment and a supportive public opinion.

A further problem with expressions of public opinion in representative democracies, as the situation stands, is that they are elicited, not interactive. Interviewees are asked what their opinions are, but have no ability to ask questions or get more information before expressing them. In this regard members of the public are passive respondents rather than active participants – forced into the role of Sartori's (1987) button-pushers as opposed to active participants in political debate. Two suggestions for enabling them to participate more have been made by Barber (1984) and Fishkin (1993) – both of them perfectly compatible with present-day representative institutions though capable of supporting a change to direct democracy if required.

Barber has suggested State backing and funding for direct popular assemblies at a series of levels which would discuss problems and policies in detail, without necessarily coming to immediate decisions on them. Indeed, one of their advantages would be the ability to accommodate deep disagreement by exercising the option to postpone decisions. This would give the opportunity for 'rich talk' about the problem rather than more obvious forms of adversarial political argument. This might well transform initial preferences on the question, eliminating the arbitrary decisions that might otherwise emerge (Miller, 1993) and focusing attention on community rather than on individual aspects of problems. In this way discussion would raise the quality of participants' judgements over the long term, as well as improving decisions (or advice, in a representative context) which would emerge from this process.

Barber's vision of these meetings is clearly inspired by American and Swiss township meetings. Critics have argued that the time and energy required to participate would render them prohibitive for ordinary individuals and hence unrepresentative, prone to take decisions from sheer exhaustion or boredom. Barber's challenge is to set them up and see who is right – himself or the critics. In a purely advisory capacity such meetings could not be dangerous and if they produced a tithe of the benefits attributed to them could be highly beneficial. On a nationwide basis they clearly have the potentiality to improve the quality of responses to the polls. Some evidence that quite ordinary people are able to sustain long discussions in order to arrive at a consensus comes from Quaker meetings over the last 300 years (Sheeran, 1983).

A more direct and economical way of informing opinion has been suggested by Fishkin and actually put into practice in a highly impressive experiment. A random sample of the British population were interviewed on the topic of justice and law and order, and their opinions recorded. They then went to a residential weekend where they had in effect a series of seminars and meetings among themselves and with experts (criminologist, judge, prison governor etc.) and representatives of political parties. At the end they were reinterviewed. Their meetings and discussions were televised nationwide.

The result of the weekend was a marked change in some attitudes, notably in regard to prison where a 59 per cent majority for more severe sentencing went down to 37 per cent after expert opinions on the inefficacy of prisons in reforming criminal behaviour were heard. On the other hand support for the reimposition of the death penalty hardly shifted, remaining almost constant at over three-quarters of the sample. (This was possibly because it was supported on purely retributive grounds rather than as a deterrent.) The experiment is reported in the *Independent* (London) of 9 May 1994. An impressive viewing figure of 8 million was attained.

This interaction of electors with experts gives some basis for evaluating criticisms of their capacity to make informed political decisions (chapter 3). It also shows how televised debates could be conducted, giving a practical model for the way they could function under direct democracy. Its immediate relevance, however, is to the question of informing public opinion under representative democracy. Clearly it does. The choice of a representative sample gives grounds for inferring what public opinion would be if everyone had the same exposure to specialists. The debates also directly inform the public through their transmission by radio and television (cf. also Arterton, 1987). They should have a considerable effect on anyone who watches them seriously, as arguments which convince the very average members of the panel might also be expected to weigh with members of the mass audience who identify with them.

Whether as an influence on the public or an indicator of their 'informed' opinion, the representative sample exposed to discussion represents an ingenious adaptation of opinion-polling which evades many of the criticisms which can be made of conceding weight to instant opinions. McLean (1989, pp. 158–60) takes the view that polls, as they simply record opinions, have a potential for evading some of the structural contradictions which may afflict voting (chapter 6). With an 'informed' sample, opinion-polling could evade criticisms of the superficiality of expressing an instant opinion to give a deeper indication of public preferences.

Referendums, public enquiries, opinion-polling and incessant media debate involving the public have all arrived in representative democracies. Barber's vision of neighbourhoods in constant political session may still seem far-fetched but the development of informed polling is just round the corner. It is important to emphasize that many of these developments are already in place, since direct democracy can so readily seem a far-fetched Utopia of some visionaries far removed from practical political life. On the contrary, the practical people are those who perceive the trends developing now and who wish to evaluate them. Like it or not, the public is already involved in debate over specific policies. Thus abstract discussions of the merits of direct and representative democracy are often covert arguments about whether existing channels of participation should be restricted or encouraged. They therefore have a very concrete relevance for the way we live, politically, in the here and now, and should be taken seriously as having direct and immediate effects.

2.8 Conclusions

This chapter has clarified the issues at stake in the theoretical confrontation between direct and representative democracy – partly by pointing out that the contrast between them is highly ambiguous and blurred. This is partly because of the central role of political parties in contemporary democracies, which would undoubtedly carry over into any viable form of direct democracy. If parties are seen as directing discussion and organizing programmes of action both in parliaments and among the populace, outcomes are not likely to differ so sharply as if we were contrasting representative decisions with unmediated popular voting *per se*.

A further reason for discounting apocalyptic visions of what change would entail is that it is already happening! Quite apart from the extreme cases where binding popular consultation over some decisions coexist with authoritative legislatures and executives, all representative democracies are much more informed and influenced by popular opinion than they were fifty years ago, largely because of technical developments in surveys and the media. The passage from expressing opinions and advice to actually voting, through a simple adaptation of existing means of consultation, would seem more a change of degree than of kind, on a broad view of current developments. Indeed, there might be relatively little difference other than terminological ones between a representative democracy reformed so as to take popular opinion fully into account, and the kind of party-based direct democracy described here. It should indeed be of relatively little concern what the formal designation is, provided that public opinion is determining on the political issues which arise.

This judgement is, however, disputed by many, from practising politicians to political theorists, as much by some with progressive orientations as by those with conservative ones. They expect any extension of popular influence which opens represenative democracy to more popular influence to have major negative effects. While politicians might automatically be expected to oppose changes which could diminish their own authority and power, their objections need to be considered seriously and answered seriously. This is even more important in the case of theorists, who have less of an obvious axe to grind. Arguments need to be taken on their merits and evaluated in terms both of their relevance (do they apply to all forms of direct democracy or only to the unmediated form?) and of their consequences (do they lead us to a rejection just of direct democracy or of democracy as such, including representative forms?).

Many criticisms of direct democracy rest in part on factual assertions about how direct democracy would work. As we have no extant system of direct democracy we cannot check out such assertions fully. We can, however, indicate where they seem arguable and when they seem to have a point. More directly, we can look at the workings of referendums and popular initiatives in those democracies that have them – some American States, Italy and Switzerland. If the involvement of a population in specific decisions produces bad effects, these ought to show themselves in referendum campaigns and outcomes.

As there are both theoretical and factual evaluations to be undertaken, we divide the task between the next two chapters. Chapter 3 reviews leading critiques of direct democracy and summarizes the counter-arguments which can be used in its favour. Chapter 4 looks at the way popular consultations work in systems which have them, focusing its analysis around various assertions that have been made about the effects and outcomes of such consultations.

Some points that have been made about direct democracy cannot really be answered until this review of popular consultations has been completed. For example, much can be made of the argument that a party-based direct democracy would evade many of the charges levelled against the unmediated form. However, a question can then be raised as to whether parties could really survive if they had to cope with popular voting on most issues rather than confining this kind of decision-making to legislatures. To cast light on this we really need to look at how Swiss, Italian and American State parties have coexisted with referendums and other forms of popular involvement. In addition, we need to give some attention to the general thesis of the decline of parties in mass democracies, especially under the impact of the media, which in time might not leave many parties around to take over the organization of direct consultations anyway!

We go on to this in chapter 5. The remaining two chapters deal in more detail with matters already discussed but which we need to consider at length – often because they are backed with an extensive literature which needs to be summarized in order to appreciate the argument to the full. This applies to the relationship between consent and voting (chapter 6), which we have to discuss before coming to general conclusions (chapter 7). All the points we shall consider are, however, introduced in the general review of arguments and counter-arguments undertaken in the next chapter.

3

New Answers to Old (and New) Criticisms

3.1 Families of Arguments

Although a lot of specific points can be made for and against direct democracy, these tend to be particular applications of general lines of argument, and thus to have a generic resemblance to each other within broad family types. Table 3.1 attempts to classify all the arguments used in this book, not just in this chapter, so we have encountered and discussed the first two (consent and feasibility) already. Similarly we do not discuss the last two sets of arguments – on the position of minorities, and the international context – but take them up later (chapter 6).

Thus the main discursive families of arguments we deal with in chapter 3 are (3) the question of the coherence and fairness of policy-making under a popular majority; (4) the capacity of ordinary people to understand, let alone decide on, complex policies; (5) the consequent need for balance between popular consent and professional expertise; and (6) a new line of argument deriving from recent rational choice analyses, that voting in any collectivity has a high probability of leading to arbitrary and unfair outcomes, which legislatures may be better able to cope with than the mass population.

These types of argument are presented in a form critical of direct democracy, because they have been developed essentially as objections to any political move in that direction. The counter-argument favouring direct democracy, or at least rebutting the criticism, is put in the second column of the table. Essentially the case against direct democracy can be summed up as saying that ordinary citizens have little political sagacity or prudence, so that they will tend to make

Table 3.1 Main types of arguments for and against direct democracy

Against	For
1. Consent and participation Elections under representative democracy already allow citizens to choose between alternative governments and programmes.	Democracy rests on the active involvement of citizens in each major decision, which is promoted to the fullest extent by direct democracy.
2. Feasibility It is not possible to have direct debate and voting in modern mass democracies.	Electronic media (TV, telephone, radio, computer) allow interactive debate and voting among physically separated citizens.
3. Tyranny of shifting majorities Without intermediary institutions (parties, legislatures, governments) no coherent policies will emerge – there will be instability, chaos and collapse of democracy. Direct democracy undermines intermediary institutions including parties.	Direct democracy does not have to be unmediated. Above all, parties and governments could play much the same role as in representative democracies today.
4. Capacity of ordinary citizens Ordinary citizens do not have the education, interest, time, expertise and other qualities required to make good political decisions.	Professional politicians do not have a monopoly of expertise and interest. In any case they could play an important part in a direct democracy through political parties and other institutions. Participation also educates and expands citizens' capacities, which are not so limited anyway. Citizens currently do spend a lot of time informing themselves about politics through TV and radio current affairs/news.

5. Balance

The system most likely to produce good decisions is one where popular participation is balanced by expert judgement. This is representative democracy where citizens can indicate the general direction policy should take but leave it to be carried out by professionals.

Expertise is important but not infallible. In any case it can be used to inform popular decisions. Present systems of representative democracy are heavily *imbalanced* against popular participation.

6. Inherent structural problems of voting

All collective decision-making can be shown mathematically to lead to arbitrary decisions in a high proportion of cases.

The problems are generic to voting procedures, so afflict representative democracy as much as direct democracy. Certain features of decision-making may, however, reduce their probability of occurrence under both systems.

7. Minorities

Those who vote against a particular decision cannot be said to give their consent to it, particularly if the same group(s) are always in the minority.

Again the problem is certainly not worse under direct democracy than under other forms of democracy. But some features of direct democracy may reduce the probability that permanent minorities emerge.

8. International context

More widespread citizen participation within States cannot affect the decisions of non-accountable bodies such as multinational corporations or world markets, which may have more important consequences for citizens than an individual government's policy.

Again this is not a criticism of direct democracy as such. The solution is the formation of world and regional governments on a democratic basis.

decisions hastily but also to be unreasonably attached to them. This will result in popular majorities being intolerant and tyrannical, a situation which can only be remedied by restricting and balancing their authority. Majority rule is also suspect because many decisions might have been different had they been voted on differently or at another time, or under different procedures which might have created an alternative majority.

The counter-arguments also group together into two or three types of rebuttal of these criticisms. A very general 'criticism of criticisms' is that they are not just against direct democracy but against democracy as such. Why consult the people at all, even to choose representatives, if they are short-sighted, unintelligent and overbearing? Is there not a likelihood that elected assemblies will share these characteristics?

Another line of reply related to this is that direct democracy may suffer from such defects but these are equally present in representative democracy – so other things being equal we would not be worse off from adopting it as a system. To this one can add that in certain ways mass participation might actually solve or ameliorate problems which afflict representative democracy, so to that extent the latter is not to be automatically preferred.

Looking at the generic lines of argument helps us see the wood before venturing into the trees. One cannot properly consider the case for and against direct democracy without going into specifics, however, so we now consider the particular arguments one by one.

3.2 Criticisms and Counter-criticisms: A General Review

To cover the full range of specific arguments, of which there are many, it is necessary to list and summarize them to some extent. For some, this is an adequate treatment. Many points have been raised by critics convinced that they had already knocked out the possibility of direct democracy with the feasibility argument. So their additional comments have been ill-considered. Once they are stated clearly it is obvious that they do not stand up – one major reason being that if accepted they would lead to rejection of democracy in *all* its forms. Other arguments are directed against unmediated mass participation but simply miss the point when applied to direct democracy with parties. A few have not properly come to terms with the saving of time and energy which comes from operating with electronic means, so they can be dismissed once this possibility is admitted.

Where criticisms have more staying power we come back to them later in the chapter. Some make a first appearance in this section, however, as it is impossible to demarcate one line of argument rigidly from another. We list them as follows:

(1) We begin with an often-used argument on the amount of time and energy which a fully participatory democracy would need in order to run properly. This is compounded by the fact that the commitment is really open-ended. The more time one side puts into political argument and lobbying activity, the more energy is consumed by the other side to counter them. At the extreme therefore everyone might have to join in full-time political activity which would be impossible to sustain, given economic, social and family demands. As a result one might see darker possibilities, such as the possibility that extremists would be the only ones with the time and inclination to stay and sway the decision in their own direction. This is the critique developed with great force by Dahl, for example, in his reflections on the student movements based on mass participation in the 1960s (Dahl, 1970, pp. 40–56) and which we have already discussed at some length in section 1.2 on the division of labour argument.

It must be said right away that this is a serious criticism of the kind of extensive face-to-face meetings advocated by Barber (1984), for example. The amount of energy and time needed for these would be great and possibly insupportable. As against this, however, four points can be made:

(i) Political debate need not be confrontational. Indeed it may have a function in resolving conflict and in persuading all concerned to adopt new common terms of reference (Miller, 1993). At least this may happen as often as it creates conflict. Where decisions are simply imposed on affected groups, as often happens in modern democracies, then indeed alienation and apathy may result. Seen as a non-conflictual activity, participation may change in character from an imposition on participants to a solidaristic and worthwhile pursuit.
(ii) This might argue in turn for structures and institutions such as businesses being reformed so as to provide individuals with more personal space for greater political activity. At a time of immense

pressures being placed on those in work, and increasing numbers outside it, such structural reforms might have beneficial economic as well as political effects. If citizens had working hours reduced by 5–10 hours a week to dedicate more time to political and civic affairs, is this self-evidently wrong?

(iii)   These points tie in to the one that Barber above all makes – that after all participation can be pleasurable, and educational. The success of night classes and of the courses of the University of the Third Age and Open University, many of them concerned with contemporary history and society, attest the fact that large sections of the population want to engage in general discussion and learning outside work. Political engagement and debate could be part of a continuous learning process.

As a footnote, one could observe that the experience of mass participation on the part of the student generations of the mid- and late 1960s does not seem to have made them worse people. Retrospectively, their opposition to Vietnam and concern with the environment seem far-sighted and sensible. What violence and terrorism was generated (on the part of very small minorities) could be seen as a reaction to the unwillingness of representative democracies to make even small concessions, rather than a consequence of mass participation as such.

(iv)   These points are debatable and indeed have formed part of the staple of debate on this subject for a long time. However, what is new and seems rather a conclusive argument against direct democracy imposing extortionate time demands on ordinary citizens is the evolution of electronically based debate and voting. Even daily votes would not seriously incommode the average citizen settling in front of the screen for evening viewing.

As for policy-related debate and discussion, it would spill over naturally from and into news and current affairs programmes. The phenomenal popularity of such programmes oriented primarily to politics (news programmes account for more than one-fifth of all viewing in Britain (HMSO, 1992, p. 178), surely testifies to an overwhelming public interest. This is closely related to entertainment. People actually enjoy current affairs and inform themselves of them as a way of passing time agreeably. Without labouring the point, general debate and discussion of issues being voted on would fit naturally into this context, and be supported by current habits and attitudes in regard to the media.

In short, the objection from time as a scarce resource misses the point, as it regards participation as an external imposition on individuals to be squeezed into a packed schedule, rather than as a diverting activity with which they *already* pass time (electronically). Combined with the other suggestions made by participation theorists, participation through the media seems relatively easy and builds naturally upon existing habits.

(2) This may all be true of the individual, so the input *to* mass participation may be assured, but what about the output *from* mass participation? Popular majorities have often been regarded as fickle and shifting, providing no basis for a permanent executive or consistent policies. Clearly this argument has a point, since if one thing emerges from comparisons of popular and parliamentary voting it is that the same disciplines cannot be applied to the former as to the latter. Decision-makers cannot count on patronage or strong ideological gratifications keeping the populace as loyal as they do their supporting legislators.

On the other hand the political parties, as pointed out in chapter 2, do organize electoral majorities and in many cases have to rely on uncertain legislative coalitions which form and reassemble round particular measures, sometimes bringing the government down with them. The US Congress and the Danish Parliament are cases in point. Reliance on popular majorities would thus not involve tremendously increased instability in many systems. This is particularly true if the safeguards built into an institutionalized and party-based form of direct democracy are introduced. It is not unreasonable that they should be and they do not detract from the 'direct' nature of the system in the sense defined above.

Fears about shifting majorities stem particularly from projects for an uninstitutionalized direct democracy in which the population not only substitutes for Parliament but to all intents and purposes for the government too. Again we have a case in which criticisms attach particularly to one type of direct democracy rather than to the concept as such. But it would hardly be fair for example to criticize the 'Westminster Model' of strict single-party majority government for failing in sensitivity to minorities, and to regard this as a conclusive criticism of representative democracy as such, ignoring the greater number of minority-sensitive coalition governments which exist under representation.

To present a balanced argument, however, we should not speak only of the limits on what popular majorities can do. For one can certainly see them as making a positive contribution to the very characteristics which make democracy an attractive political system. If majorities do shift it is not necessarily because they are inherently fickle but because they are communicating something about policies: either that different problems are coming to the fore or that the government is not tackling current ones. In either case it is surely good that they should communicate the message. Institutional arrangements can be built in to ensure that the government has a reasonable stability. But if it persists in going consistently counter to majority wishes over a longer time period, should it not be forced to demit?

One can indeed shift perspective and change the terminology from majorities being fickle to governments being unresponsive. It is clear that in many types of representative system, whether 'Westminster' types often elected by a minority anyway, coalitions formed in direct contravention of election results, or executives elected for a fixed term, many measures are taken which are far-reaching, immensely disruptive to individuals and widely unpopular (Vietnam, or the British poll tax of 1989–93, for example). Is it not right, in democratic terms, that citizens should be able to react directly to these? The stock answer, that governments need to be able to take unpopular measures for the general good (which they know better than the population) invites the reply that in that case their superior wisdom should not have to be tempered by electoral considerations every four to five years. Criticism of popular unreliability, in other words, runs close to criticism of democracy in any form: if one cannot trust popular voting on particular measures, why should one trust it to choose the governors?

(3)   This is often the juncture at which considerations of balance get raised. Popular voting may be shifting and unstable; however, it does provide messages to governments about popular reactions to their policies, which the prospect of a coming election forces them to take into account. The development of public opinion polls provides continuing evidence about popular reactions which was hard to get in the past; so do phone-ins and chat-shows. Representative democracy from this point of view has accommodated modern developments in information technology and pre-empted the need to get popular consent. In this way it can balance the necessarily uninformed and inconsistent reactions of the public with the expertise of legislators and party politicians, to get a blend of responsive but also informed

and firm decision-making. It is in this sense that it constitutes a superior system to any in which one of these elements gets out of hand.

The point that virtue is found in balancing different political elements in the Constitution goes back to Aristotle (1958, pp. 172–90) and more recently Madison (1787–8/1911, pp. 41–8). One could argue, however, that the party-based forms essential to the working of representative democracy today are hardly in the middle of a continuum but are tilted against popular involvement, allowing general popular reactions only a little chink to let themselves, possibly, be felt. The existence of a legislative buffer and infrequent elections in conjunction with a competitive party system puts a positive premium on manipulating public opinion and voting, by altering policy in the run-up to the election in order to produce prosperity and gain another term, then imposing unpopular measures immediately afterwards when elections are far away (Tufte, 1978; Margolis and Mauser, 1989).

The difficulty with public opinion, as participatory theories often argue, is that, if it is irresponsible and uninformed, this is because one is asked to make judgements without debate, and express opinions without immediate responsibility for the way they will affect oneself and one's associates. If it is necessary to emasculate expressions of popular opinion and to build so many safeguards against them, why again is it necessary to have them at all? Or, if they provide essential information, why not substitute polls for elections, since wise representatives and politicians will take popular opinions into account anyway? What is the unique virtue of elections if they simply tempt politicians from their considered courses of action, which are better for everyone than simply pandering to popular whims?

(4) If the special expertise of political professionals is discounted, however, would the institution of direct democracy (as distinct from the impact of the mass media as such) not destroy the political parties? These are often criticized from a participatory viewpoint as diverting and manipulating the popular will. Would any system of direct democracy not necessarily do without them, or at least weaken them, thus knocking out the major modern political innovation which organizes and forms opinion and helps it operate responsibly?

We have already tackled this question in chapter 2. A direct, unmediated form of direct democracy would indeed knock out the parties, like every other political institution and constraint. But, as I have argued before, this is not the only form direct democracy need take. In a pragmatically organized direct democracy parties would be invaluable for the purposes of focusing opinion and guaranteeing implementation just as they are in representative democracy. The critique just made of parties, as legislative buffers against popular reactions, is of their operation in the particular case of representative democracy with occasional elections and does not relate to what they might do were they made continuingly responsive to popular reactions.

(5)   Mention of the parties brings us to the role of the professional politicians manning them, the men and women living off as well as for politics in Weber's sense (Weber, 1958; Mastropaolo, 1993, pp. 19–56). Distrusted as full-time organizers of conflict and agitators till the early twentieth century, they have come to be seen as equally essential to politics as their counterparts in the economic sphere – speculators, financiers and entrepreneurs – to the smooth operation of the market. And for the same reasons: they are the people who, to take their profits, persuade, organize and get things done, smooth the way to bills and administrative measures, bring together disparate groups, often creating a consensus but in any case facilitating the collective action which would otherwise not be undertaken (Olson, 1965).

Granting all these points, it follows from what has been said about parties that professionals can still play an important role in institutionalized forms of direct democracy (if not also in formally unmediated forms – even the Athenians had Pericles). Popular voting would require facilitators more, if anything, than legislative voting. Only, they might be more wary of becoming obliged to special interests when operating in a public arena.

(6)   Or perhaps not. One argument often brought against popular voting, even in representative systems, is that it is ill-informed and apathetic. Would this not lead to a situation in which, after the first novelty wore off, 'popular voting' actually degenerated to voting by small self-interested groups very open to manipulation by professionals with an axe to grind? Something of the sort often seems to happen with certain contemporary referendums, again California being taken as a worst possible case (even if Proposition 65, which attacked vested interests, did pass in 1986, cf. chapter 4 below).

While domination by selfish interests is a clear danger, it is not necessarily insuperable, for the following reasons:

(i)   Where parties retain a role, it is in their interest to organize the vote and stimulate turnout and argument – in short to do all the things that parties normally do under present systems of representation.

(ii)   A minimum voting level could be required for measures to pass. This would make it even more important for parties to stimulate participation.

(iii)   From a participatory point of view greater opportunities for debate and participation stimulate greater engagement. Representative democracy can well be seen as institutionalizing popular inertia through its limitation of such opportunities. It would be unwise to claim there would be a magical transformation of popular attitudes after the extension of public debate and voting on policies but, combined with suitable civic programmes in schools and colleges and the opportunities offered for 'electronic' participation, some increase in popular attention and interest is surely to be expected.

(iv)   Voting could of course be compulsory. Far from 'forcing people to be free', this has been a feature of many post-war representative democracies (Italy, the Netherlands, Belgium). Of course compulsory voting once every four years is a different matter from voting weekly or monthly, but the use of electronic means substantially reduces the costs involved.

(7)   This, however, immediately opens the way to another criticism of direct participation – *should* decisions be swayed by the views of uninformed apathetics, pushed into voting solely by coercion? Does not this immediately discredit all the claims of direct democracy to higher moral standing? Does it not clearly demonstrate the superior merits of representative democracy where decisions can be made by informed professionals able to assess the arguments of specialists properly and to handle them correctly (Sartori, 1987, pp. 431–9)?

   Here is perhaps the nub of the whole argument against direct democracy: the mass of the citizens are not qualified to decide high policy, so they can be allowed to influence it only indirectly, by choosing those who are to decide rather than deciding themselves. This objection can be considered from several aspects. In the first place there is a contrast between individual qualities and collective decision-making. This is considered below. In the second place there is the question of the rights of the ill-informed. For example – is it self-evident that they should be excluded from decision-making for the whole society which includes themselves? Thirdly, the terms of the question itself should be examined – what is meant by knowledge and information in the political context? We consider each of these three points under separate heads below:

(i)   It is of course by no means clear that politicians and legislators are invariably well informed. The mode by which legislators specialize in different areas, and defer to each others' opinions in areas where they are ignorant, is well known (Matthews, 1973, p. 32). The list of political blunders and errors, from the creation of vast deserts of concrete housing lacking elementary support facilities, to the food surpluses and disruptive effects of the European common agricultural policy, by way of colossal cost over-runs or blatant mistreatment of minorities inside many programmes, is enough to call in doubt any claim to superior wisdom. It is the self-corrective built in through its tolerance of debate and argument that makes democracy a superior political system. But in that case where is the objection to extending it?

Clearly on an overall, average comparison, legislators will show up as more generally informed and politically aware than the average citizen. However, there is an important distinction between the individuals involved and the collective process which leads to decision. The individual competence of the legislator hardly counts in representative systems with strict party voting: what matters are the capacities of the party leadership.

In a direct democracy with parties, therefore, the quality of decision-making would hardly vary from that of current Parliaments, both depending heavily on the guidance of the party leadership. Parties would have more difficulty getting popular majorities for their policy, but not insuperable ones. Indeed, the necessity of meeting and overcoming wider criticism and debate might even improve the quality of the policies initially put forward. While the proportions of the educated, informed and politically engaged in the population are clearly lower than in the legislature, the absolute numbers are of course vastly greater. On the argument that the quality of a decision is improved by greater expertise, opening it up to participation by more experts should surely help. (On the extensive survey evidence for the general stability and reasonableness of collective public opinion, see Page and Shapiro, 1993.)

These points are supported by evidence from Cronin's comprehensive analysis of the operation and results of popular referendums in the United States. These, he concludes, have 'generally been used in a reasonable and constructive manner', have 'almost always rejected extreme proposals', and citizens 'have generally acted in an enlightened manner and have not threatened minority rights' (1989, pp. 197–8, 212–14). We shall examine his evidence in relation to other accounts of these processes in the next chapter. But it makes a prima-facie case for popular majorities not necessarily being rash and ignorant. This point is also supported by the most recent analyses of American survey evidence on popular attitudes and opinions (Marcus and Hanson, 1993).

(ii)   Wider popular participation certainly means that large numbers of ill-informed, unsophisticated elements in the population will also be given access to the debate. Some commentators have taken this as such a self-evident defect of proposals for direct democracy as to invalidate it from the start (Sartori, 1987, pp. 116–18). Better a representative system in which popular opinion can be read off from polls and entered as an element into the decision by professionals, rather than one in which the ignorant can directly affect policies. They have no moral right to participation and could only degrade the quality of the decisions.

Taking the last point first, it does rather assume that no important decisions are ever taken by majorities of ignorant legislators and that the quality of current decision-making *could* be significantly lowered within a continuing democratic context. Cronin (1989, pp. 210–11) finds no evidence from the US States that popular decisions are any worse than legislative ones. If parties continue as prime movers so that policy is essentially party policy, participation by the uneducated and unsophisticated is unlikely to downgrade the quality of decisions.

A wider question is that of their right to participation. Should the ignorant be *ipso facto* excluded from political decisions bearing upon them? The justification for doing so surely rests on some idea of their own and society's best interests being served by this – a generally better decision will be reached without them.

However, this ignores two significant considerations. In the first place political ignorance is not a static quality: people can be educated, and educated through debate (Barber, 1984, p. 232; Miller, 1993). This is shown dramatically in the televised experiment already discussed, where a representative sample of ordinary people were put through a series of televised seminars with experts. The interest aroused by making decisions on matters touching their immediate well-being is likely to increase the motivation for learning even on the part of disadvantaged sections.

Secondly, the definitions of general interest and 'best interest of a specified group' are problematic and debatable, and shaped by the perceived interests of those making the decision. One justification of the extension of rights to all, and also of pluralistic interpretations of democracy, is that all groups should have a voice to ensure that the decision reflects something of everyone's interests. As the uneducated, ignorant and unsophisticated are unevenly distributed over social groups, they are very likely to lose out by their exclusion (Parry, 1989).

Advocates of representation point out that such groups are able to vote for parties under existing democratic forms and that this gives them a certain leverage – but at the same time the party and legislative buffer prevents them destabilizing or rendering inconsistent the content of decisions. Again, however, these terms themselves are hardly fixed objectively: what may be stability and consistency to those whose interests are served by current decisions may be unemployment and discrimination to those excluded from them. Moreover, apathy is more likely to represent a negative protest against the political set-up than acquiescence in it; hence it reflects and to some extent creates the alienation feared by many theorists of mass society (Kornhauser, 1960, pp. 108–28).

Once again the argument against direct democracy in this context lends itself easily to general anti-democratic stances. If certain elements should be excluded from direct decision-making because of ignorance, why should they even participate in the selection of decision-makers? And if there are arguments for them choosing decision-makers, are these not the same arguments for them contributing to decisions?

(iii)   The point has been made above that many political concepts, particularly concepts of interest, are themselves debatable. Here we should underline that terms like 'political ignorance' and 'expertise', 'uneducated', 'unsophisticated' and 'apathetic' are all controvertible from differing points of view. This is particularly true when they are regarded as static and unresponsive to changes in political circumstances. As I shall expand on this point in a later section it is only necessary to summarize it here, underlining one particular consequence. Accepting that personal characteristics are not static and that they change with political circumstances is to accept the thesis of participatory theorists that an extension of opportunities will itself change the political nature of many citizens from apathy and lack of interest, which produce withdrawal and ignorance, to involvement and interest, which produce more sophistication and information.

One need not go all the way with those who regard participation as a universal political panacea to see that it could have a certain motivating and educational effect.

Two general conclusions which emerge from these arguments and counter-arguments are that:

1   Arguments against direct democracy are usually directed against its plebiscitory, unmediated, uninstitutionalized form. They do not hold against direct voting guided and organized by the political parties, which is the most likely form it would take in contemporary societies.

2   Arguments against direct democracy, particularly in its uninstitutionalized form, have a habit of turning into arguments against representative democracy as well, since it is difficult to argue against direct policy involvement without casting aspersions on citizens' political abilities. The question then becomes: if they are themselves so bad at making decisions, why should they be allowed to decide on who *is* to make them? If this is answered in terms of elections making parties responsive, the counter-question is: why should they not be more responsive? It is hard to find arguments that discriminate between direct and representative democracy, rather than between democracy and less responsive systems, other than in terms of balance. But why should the balance stop where it does? Why should it not go on to more direct forms, particularly if major institutional features like political parties are retained?

The major argument to the contrary was formulated by James Madison in Paper X of *The Federalist Papers* (1787–8/1911), which can be summarized by saying that representation provides a 'filter' for popular opinion by subjecting it to deliberation and decision by the 'best' men, thus ameliorating its tendency to prejudice, passion and impulse. At bottom this is what most who see positive merits in representative democracy are implying, so the argument needs to be taken further in the next section and considered more deeply.

Many points have been taken as far as they can be in this review. But two other major arguments not considered adequately above require more extended treatment. These cover the other grounds on which so many criticisms of direct democracy base themselves: the lack of information and expertise of the public, which render their opinions on many subjects quite valueless. Section 3.4 looks more closely at what is meant by the terms 'informed' and 'ignorant' and the role of professionals and experts as compared to the average citizen. Section 3.5 builds on the previous discussions, by asking whether publics are inherently confined to reviewing personalities and past record rather than voting on policy-alternatives, because of an inbuilt instability in their decision-processes.

3.3 Representation as Filter: The Madisonian Argument

The most vigorous defence of representation as valid in its own right comes from James Madison (1787–8/1911, pp. 41–7, 263–7). Madison's argument starts with the desirability of thwarting the wishes of factions (who may constitute the majority), as these are mostly selfish and opposed to the general interest. Factional predominance has produced the hasty and unwise decisions of popular assemblies, while factional conflict has rendered them shifting and inconsistent.

As factions cannot be eliminated except by force, a free society has to live with them but at the same time moderate them. One way is by putting power into the hands of representatives, who are more likely to be aware of the long-term interests of the population than the population itself. Permitting citizens to vote on who represents them guarantees accountability and thus secures control over the representatives. But the representatives in turn come between the people and their wishes with their own critical political judgement, thus insulating public policy from their passions. (Indeed a double barrier is set up as representatives in the various government institutions need to concur for policy to be effective.)

Madison's arguments repeat many of the points reviewed above, but put them together in a unique and original synthesis. His position is a compelling one but is subject to equally forceful counter-arguments, particularly in view of modern developments:

(1)   Few modern democrats would argue against the need for political parties to organize and focus governments and elections. Yet these are the very 'factions' Madison fears. A party voted in by a popular majority can in contemporary representative democracies do more or less what it likes (even in the United States, in spite of its separated legislative and executive powers (Budge and Hofferbert, 1990)). Madisonian arguments are simply outmoded by this development. Party control has destroyed the checks and balances he had in mind, and yet is clearly essential to the functioning of the system in modern times. Direct democracy would paradoxically impose more checks on the majority party's will than representative democracies now do.

(2) Madisonian arguments are also outmoded in another way. In the eighteenth and early nineteenth century legislators themselves constituted a significant part of the educated elite, with most of which they were linked in one way or another. When one talked of legislative 'filtering' therefore one was talking of a task performed by almost all of the educated and informed people in society, in contrast to the uneducated and highly localized and parochial masses.

The situation today is very different. The most highly educated are not even in the legislatures nor even closely connected with them. Instead they are in the media or the universities. Persons of wealth and position are in business. The balance has shifted so that to exclude the population from direct decision-making is also to exclude the most educated and those arguably best able to deliberate and decide. Representation may thus have directly opposite effects to those argued by Madison in actually excluding most persons of position and education from decision-making.

(3) Cronin's sustained research on direct popular participation in referendums (1989, p. 198) shows that voters judge shrewdly and are at least as competent as the corresponding legislators. They show little sign of being swayed by partial passions. The common reaction when unsure about or confused by a referendum item is to opt for the status quo (cf. chapter 4 below). Both systematic analysis (Cronin, 1989; Marcus and Hanson, 1993), and historical accounts (Smout, 1984) stress the moderation and pragmatism of popular movements since the Industrial Revolution, even though they were often spurred on by appalling conditions. Historical episodes like the French Revolution or the rise of the Nazis reflect the weakness and bankruptcy of ruling elites rather than the passions of the people (and in the last Weimar election a popular majority voted against the Nazis). Given this, enhanced popular participation might seem a bulwark for democracy rather than a threat to it.

3.4 'Information' and 'Expertise' as Criteria for Policy-participation

Modern developments therefore seem to have turned Madison on his head. If we want to involve the 'best' in decision-making we *need* to open it up to the population. However, a major argument of authors as disparate in other respects as Schumpeter (1950, p. 263), Plamenatz (1973, p. 194) and Sartori (1987, pp. 115–20) is that most citizens who would thus be let in to decision-making are incapable of making everyday political decisions and should for that reason be confined to passing judgements on their representatives in elections. The reasons for this vary: for Schumpeter it is their total lack of interest and involvement in politics; for Plamenatz it is the different criteria used by voters in deciding between parties compared to the expertise involved in decisions (one may sensibly choose between solicitors in complete ignorance of law); for Sartori it is the extreme technicality of political problems which make them difficult for professional politicians let alone ordinary citizens to understand (1987, 431–4). These observations may all be regarded as updating aspects of Madison's argument in line with modern conditions and hence deserve consideration on their own account.

While the various reasons given for excluding citizens from specific decision-making vary, they are not contradictory and are indeed in some ways are mutually reinforcing. Lack of interest in the public sphere removes a major motivation for acquiring knowledge; this may well then lead to citizens making decisions on different criteria from those used by legislators. Sartori's criticism of the cognitive incompetence of ordinary citizens is more forceful in that it is seen as irremediable, given the complexity of modern decisions and their susceptibility only to technical and expert analysis. Experts are *de facto* acquiring more power, or at least more standing and influence than ever before, and on this ground alone it is inappropriate to argue for more direct citizen judgements on policy (Sartori, 1987, pp. 432–5). (But see the conflicting research evidence in Marcus and Hanson, 1993.)

Two answers can be given to this line of argument:

(1)   Parry (1989) suggests that knowledge is not of one piece and therefore cannot be the monopoly of one group of specialists. (See also Dahl, 1989, pp. 67–9, 349 n. 5.) There is no one objective assessment to be made of nuclear risk, for example: the standard basis of comparison – number of past deaths per unit of output – can be challenged on the grounds that future conditions (and generating plants) are different from those in the past, so deaths cannot be projected. The nuclear industry as a whole is a good example of highly challengeable assumptions made by specialists which have been shown to be matters of opinion more than anything else. British nuclear generating costs were for many years shown as cheaper than

those of conventional fuel. This, however, was because they were based on the first-generation Magnox stations, pushed many of the initial research and development costs on to the military nuclear programme, and ignored the prospects of increasing breakdown with age and ultimate decommissioning. Only when private business refused to purchase the nuclear part of the industry were alternative cost estimates made (as had been consistently urged by environmentalists and coal-miners).

These examples demonstrate that the unchallengeability of technical judgements is itself an element of political debate and subject to challenge. The relatively uninformed may not be able to make technical judgements directly, owing to their lack of relevant expertise, but they can always find or hire their own experts to challenge the original judgement and to suggest alternative tests or criteria. Sartori's view on the inevitable prevalence of technical experts ignores the fact that science and engineering are not closed bodies of knowledge. They are very open to new ideas and to debate.

Thus the claim that there is a hermetically sealed body of expert knowledge that overrides political judgement is itself an element in political debate and can always be queried. This frees political professionals from subordination to experts. And what it does for them it does also for average citizens, with their increasing access to media channels tuned in to debates between experts, documentaries and educational programmes. Far from being relatively less informed than in the past, the citizen is, *vis-à-vis* specialists and professionals, better informed.

(2)   A second argument used by Barber (1988, pp. 199–211) is that public judgement on technical points comes into play only where experts disagree. If they are unanimous, citizens can vote on the matter without needing specialist knowledge (we know smoking harms health: should we then ban it or leave it to individual decision? – a purely political judgement). Where experts disagree about consequences, as on some aspects of genetic engineering or nuclear power, the public has to make a judgement in the area. But this is less a technical decision and more of a political evaluation: are the levels of risk tolerable compared to likely benefits? As pointed out above, the public's assessment of risk may differ from experts', but is not for that reason wrong.

Ordinary citizens may well of course simplify decisions through devices like those specified by Plamenatz (1973, p. 194). They will for example project the past behaviour and ideology of a party on to what they might do in an unpredictable future: thus a vote for a left-wing party might be given, not on the basis of what it currently promises to do, but on the projection that, whatever happens, it will always keep up levels of welfare more than its rival(s) (Budge and Farlie, 1983, p. 30).

Plamenatz interprets this as a different form and basis of judgement from that applied by the political elite, though not less rational. Given the complexity and volume of the information available, however, it is clear that everyone must use calculating and simplifying rules of this kind. The specialist cannot be equally expert over the whole of his or her narrow field, still less over the whole of science. An easy way to decide on the balance of probabilities for a particular finding in a vaguely known but relevant field is to count the relative frequency of findings on the one side as opposed to others – hardly much different from the citizen adding up salient issues which 'belong' to one party or another and voting for the one with the largest number of preferred positions. The politicians consistently voting for the party position in legislatures on the grounds that it is probably right in areas outside their own expertise are using another simplifying rule. Nobody can operate without such rules – not even scientists with citation indices.

Citizen ignorance and inconsistency are often summed up in an example (McLean, 1989, p. 109). A majority of electors wanted tax cuts at the same time as a majority wanted welfare increased. Both alternatives were clearly endorsed by a majority. This can be interpreted as political naiveté – how else could welfare be paid for but by tax increases? To this an informed answer might be – by defence cuts, inflation, joining the European Union, foreign aid and economic growth. There are a lot of strategies, any or all of which might be pursued, but pervasive uncertainty about which might work.

Electors are after all not so naive. It is the tendency of experts and professional politicians to codify knowledge, to pretend or convince themselves that there is only one possible course of action, which makes them appear so – though often of course this is a political strategy of politicians to impose a solution rather than evidencing lack of sophistication on the part of citizens. Sophistication is usually measured in the way survey specialists define it, which often enshrines a partial and far from objective conception of what it is.

Simplified calculating strategies are used at all levels, not just that of electors; they are not products of ignorance and lack of sophistication but rational ways of coping with a complex and confusing world. Knowledge is not static but subject both to expansion and change from general discussion. The latter is much less likely to impoverish than to enrich it.

3.5 Voting Cycles, Instability and Majority Decisions: A 'Brick Wall' for Direct Democracy?

In discussing differences in knowledge and information between citizens and their representatives Sartori (1987, pp. 106–10) makes the (highly controvertible) point that the former have unstable opinions on most general matters but enough personal experience of how they themselves and the groups with which they identify are doing under a government to judge the representatives' performance. We have dealt with some of the relevant arguments above. By a somewhat different route two other authors (Riker, 1982; McLean, 1989) have arrived at essentially the same conclusion, drawing on social choice theory. We need to consider their argument because if popular voting on policies, no matter how well-informed, is inherently unstable and shifting, and thus unable to reflect true majority opinion, this is clearly a conclusive rebuttal of the possibility of direct democracy even in the institutionalized form which we have been mainly discussing.

The argument takes its start from the well-known voting cycle phenomenon (Condorcet, 1785; Arrow, 1951). Succinctly put, the theorem states: 'a rational individual who prefers A to B to C must prefer A to C . . . it is always possible that majority rule is intransitive. In the simplest case, if voter 1 prefers A to B and B to C, voter 2 prefers C to A and A to B, and voter 3 prefers B to C and C to A, there is a majority for A over B, a majority for B over C, and a majority for C over A. Transitive individual preferences lead to an intransitive social ordering, otherwise known as a cycle' (McLean, 1991, p. 506).

It is easy to see how this pattern of voting might generalize over large populations, and how it could occur often enough to cast doubt on the pretension of any popular vote to reflect true majority opinion (McLean, 1989, p. 123). It would be equally likely, on the basis of these arguments, to reflect an arbitrary placement of topics on the agenda, or even deliberate manipulation of it.

McLean uses this argument as proof that the new electronic technology and a direct democracy based upon it will not overcome this inherent problem of voting procedures as such. Clearly, if we accept the inevitability of its occurrence in democratic voting processes, this point is correct. His discussion, however, concentrates upon *mass* voting and participation in relation to the possibility of its occurrence. This leaves the impression that in some way it is more likely to occur under direct than under representative democracy. But in fact, as McLean himself notes (McLean 1989, pp. 123–4) an increase in numbers voting does not raise the probability of its occurrence notably compared to an increase in the number of options being considered.

While he does not say so explicitly, the overall impression left by his discussion is that direct democracy at national level is unattainable, as it could provide no guarantees against the occurrence of cycles (McLean, 1989, p. 135). Riker on the other hand makes the explicit argument that popular voting is best confined to passing judgement on the representatives' record, as this does not involve cycles (Riker, 1982, pp. 1–25, 97–118). In this sense both support Sartori (1987, pp. 106–20), Schumpeter (1950, p. 263) and Plamenatz (1970, p. 194), who reach the same conclusion on the basis of the citizens' limited inherent capacities for political decision-making. It is indeed clear that to support representative democracy against direct democracy on the one hand and against more authoritarian alternatives on the other, one has to argue, even from relatively diverse initial premises, to a similar conclusion: citizens are capable of judging representatives but not of deciding policy. The argument from inherent limitations on intellectual capacity having been shown to be debatable, the one from cycles and inability to find a true majority emerges as crucial.

The problem, however, not recognized in these discussions is that it seems to apply with relatively equal force to legislative decisions. If the act of voting by itself generates inherent and unresolvable problems of arbitrariness and instability, this is going to apply to legislators as much as to populations.

It is true that various authors have pointed to institutional arrangements which may ameliorate the problem. For example, it has been suggested that legislatures divide policy into a number of separate areas and consider each individually through their committee structure, partly because this brings only one set of considerations into play at any one time. This separates out policy decisions and implies that on any one area there will be a unidimensional structure of opinion which makes it possible to find a fair and stable compromise between opposing opinions at the position of the median legislator. Taking a simple example, if almost half wanted to spend more on defence and almost half less, it would not be unfair to settle on the current level of spending. As everybody would see this was the best they could hope to get on defence spending given other people's opinions, the decision would not be changed later on (Shepsle and Weingast, 1981).

A similar outcome would hold with other policy areas like education, environment and so on – *if* they were separated out from each other. If they were put together, so that decisions on education depended partly on what was done on defence, then the final outcome in each issue-area would differ from what it would be if these policies were discussed separately – it would not be the position at the median of each issue-dimension. But then it would not be stable either.

An advantage urged for legislatures is that this structuring of policy-areas, which they impose though their procedures and structures, does enable them to evade cycles. However, it could also be urged on behalf of direct democracy that (1) courts would rule that each separate issue should be put separately to the population as they already do with referendums (Butler and Ranney, 1994); (2) that citizens would naturally tend to view issue-areas as separable in this way in order to impose a necessary simplicity on their decisions. There are no obvious connections between such areas as defence, education and environment. Therefore they are likely to consider them separately (Budge and Farlie 1983, pp. 22–6) and avoid cycles (Ordeshook 1986, p. 250) just as legislators do.

There are other points to consider: for example, would legislators vote in a more strategic way than electors, lying about their preferences and bargaining to get a favourable result? Many of these points require supporting technical and background discussion, so we consider them in more detail in chapter 6, which examines the nature of debate and voting more closely.

A last point, however, can be made non-technically. Schofield (1985, pp. 292–9) has pointed out that forming a majority judgement about how government has performed involves much the same possibilities of voting cycles as does the formulation of preferences on a particular issue. Distributions over three judgements – the government has performed, well, indifferently or badly – could involve as much of a Condorcet cycle as deciding between issue preferences. This seems a conclusive argument against any attempt to attribute more inherent difficulties to direct popular voting on policies than on the election of representatives. The attempt to mobilize social choice theory against direct democracy encounters the familiar pitfall of arguing against the possibility of democracy as such, even in regard to retrospective evaluation of records, rather than against any particular form of it.

3.6 Conclusions

What this general review seems to show is that direct democracy cannot now be dismissed on grounds of impracticability alone, given increasing opportunities for two-way communication between citizen and citizen, citizen and opinion-former, and between citizens and governments. Unmediated voting with the citizenry acting as both legislature and executive is not the only form that it need take: there is no reason why popular voting should not be guided and organized by political parties just as legislative voting is now. Recognition of this last possibility subverts many arguments against direct democracy. Those which survive take on a radical tinge, tipping over into a critique of citizens' (and even politicians') capacity for making any informed collective decision at all – an argument which in the end ranges them against representative democracy as much as against direct democracy.

In particular, the attempt to draw a strict barrier between specialists' knowledge and that of the ordinary person seems based on a static and utopian conception of specialist knowledge which is essentially untenable in light of modern evidence. Voting cycles, if they exist in practice, apply to all voting processes and not just popular ones.

The discussion demonstrates that better and more refined arguments need to be found against direct democracy if they are to stick. Perhaps more importantly, however, it suggests the main gulf lies between supporters of democracy as such and supporters of elitist and other alternatives. This is a point to be taken up in chapter 7 below.

We cannot regard the debate as concluded at this stage. A substantial role in the evaluation of arguments on both sides of the debate has been played by factual assertions about how direct democracy would operate once it was introduced. These cry out to be checked against some evidence to see if they are true or not. Can we expect disaster from moves to mass participation? Or does it on the contrary improve the quality of debate and policy outputs? How well do parties cope? Even if the evidence is mixed, we can learn something from the experience of polities which have tried to extend the scope for mass participation through referendums and initiatives.

In chapter 4 we accordingly look at the systems – some US States and Swiss cantons, Federal Switzerland itself and Italy – which, though representative democracies, have allowed popular votes to count on important issues. We are interested both in the processes and outcomes of popular decision-making, and in how these have affected political parties, which have been cited at many points in this chapter as guarantors of stability and coherence in a mediated form of direct democracy.

4

Participation in Practice

4.1 Preliminary Considerations

Direct popular voting on important policy decisions is far from being a novelty in the world. Despite theorists' standard dismissal of the possibility of a popular assembly, policy-consultations of the whole electorate have been held since the early nineteenth century in many countries. These increased in number under the impetus of radical and reforming movements in the early twentieth century; and they experienced a new expansion in the second half of the post-war era.

Voting in these consultations has been based predominantly on the print and postal technology of the nineteenth century and has not rested on the technological advances discussed in chapter 1. So it hardly reflects the fluidity and capacity for long-distance interaction which new developments bestow. In other ways too the legal and institutional framework created for consultations render popular re-actions to them a very distant reflection of what they might be under other circumstances. The form they take on cannot therefore be regarded as conclusive evidence for the superiority either of representative or direct democracy, in terms of the arguments we have been assessing in the previous chapter. The actual functioning of referendums and initiatives is most valuable probably in ruling out some of the more extreme claims on either side. This is, however, useful – especially for a discussion which aims to put the debate about direct democracy on a clear footing rather than to settle it definitively one way or another.

One point about the policy consultations we shall consider is especially relevant to the arguments put forward previously. That is, being spurred on by the ideal of unmediated popular voting discussed in chapter 2 (particularly in the United States), they were often instituted to attack or undermine the influence of political parties, which were seen as selfish and corrupt representatives of special interests. This faith in an unmediated expression of the popular will has been especially potent and appealing for supporters of direct democracy, even if it is not the only viable form in which that system can be institutionalized.

As a result of this historical inheritance parties have often been excluded, by convention or habit, from organizing or guiding voting, particularly on popular initiatives. Where referendums are an occasional device for passing legislation normally put through Parliament, parties additionally may employ them to decide on issues where they themselves are deeply divided internally (not a stance which would be possible were popular voting the normal mode of decision).

As a result of both these tendencies we are not in a position to evaluate directly how parties would function under a full-blown direct democracy with possibly very different practices from those that exist now. We can, however, make inferences about whether *any* extension of direct democracy is basically incompatible with healthy parties and shall go on to evaluate these in chapter 5, focusing here on the actual ways in which referendums and initiatives operate under the present set-up.

4.2 Direct Participation in Policy-making around the World

This said, actual experience with referendums and other forms of direct participation does form the only way of evaluating many of the arguments about direct democracy from a practical rather than from a purely theoretical and speculative standpoint. We start with a general review of experiences with popular intervention around the world, before going on to specific countries.

Most democratic systems have had some experience of popular policy voting. This tends, however, to have been severely limited both in scope – to constitutional and moral matters – and in frequency, partly because such consultations cannot be initiated by popular petition but only by some constitutionally constituted authority, the legislature or Presidency. Technically, most countries hold *referendums* called by governments, rather than *initiatives* called by a group among the electorate. This immediately gives them a special character, most notably their tendency to be held on subjects on which the parties themselves cannot agree internally. The three cases where consultations can be called by non-official bodies are in about half the American States, in Switzerland at Federal, Cantonal and Communal levels, and in Italy. Because of the greater scope thereby allowed to popular voting we consider each of these cases separately below, reviewing here experiences with and results of referendums in other countries.

Referendums are generally held on two types of subject. The first are constitutional changes, including also questions of territorial adjustment. The recent series of referendums on accession to the European Union, and on endorsements to extensions to the founding treaties, neatly cover both aspects in the member countries. After the breakdown of Communism in Central and Eastern Europe, the new democratic constitution was in many cases also voted on by the people at large.

Such consultations are often mandated by the constitution itself, by way of emphasizing its special status above normal law-making provision and rendering it particularly difficult to change without a general consensus. However, constitutions are rarely changed in their entirety, and whether a particular proposal actually entails constitutional change is often a matter of (highly political) judgement. In France, for example, General de Gaulle called many more referendums as President in the 1960s than any of his predecessors have done since. While these involved such central changes as direct election of the President, the equally 'constitutional' question of the method of election of the popular house of parliament in the 1980s was not based on a referendum (Bogdanor, 1994, pp. 56–61).

This element of political judgement assimilates 'constitutional' referendums to those held on other subjects, which again involve calculations of political advantage on the part of governments or Presidents (and hence by political parties). The other area in which consultations are frequently held is that of moral and social issues, often pitting traditional morality against the right of individual choice, but extending as far as environmental planning and nuclear power.

What these issues have in common is that they are often not covered by the ideology of established parties, particularly if that is based primarily on class and redistributive questions. Thus they raise threats of internal factionalism and splits. To avoid this, leaders of normally hostile parties have a common interest in agreeing on a referendum, evading intra-party conflict by allowing all sectors a free voice in expressing their opinions, and defining the conflict as a non-partisan one.

The exceptions to this general rule are Christian or religious parties, where they exist, central to whose ideology is the defence of traditional morality against individual choice on matters such as divorce or abortion. As they are generally fighting to preserve a traditionalist status quo, their unity is likely to be affirmed rather than impaired on the issue. Thus they are disposed to resist the resort to a referendum in the first place and to fight it as a unified force if it takes place.

Unity is also the norm for Green parties on environmental or nuclear issues. Both Green ideology and political interest would favour a referendum, however, which is more likely to overturn established pro-business policy than normal parliamentary proceedings. The same is true of minority nationalist or regionalist parties seeking to demonstrate widespread local support for autonomy or secession.

Referendums therefore are not free from partisan influences even though many parties may seek to avoid taking an official stand upon them (or in the case of constitutional questions, may all seek to take the same stand). They may often contribute to the defeat or weakening of established parties. This may be due to the effect of party members allying across partisan boundaries to form a coalition with members of the opposition on the subject of the referendum, raising the possibility of new political alliances emerging out of that issue. Or it could result from a new party united on the issue gaining a political success and using it to establish political credibility with electors. This could lead to vote gains at the next parliamentary election and even a place in a coalition government.

However, one should be wary of interpreting these effects as demonstrating the anti-party bias of popular consultations as such. First, they as often provide established parties with a way of avoiding splits as exacerbating them. Secondly, they are often useful occasions for new and anti-establishment parties to promote themselves. This is hardly consistent with the idea that all parties are necessarily weakened by popular consultation. This is only the case if *established* parties are taken as synonymous with *all* parties. Although this equation of the two is commonly made, particularly by spokespersons of the parties affected, it only needs to be pointed out to be exposed as spurious. Green and New Politics parties are just as much parties as Christians, Conservatives, Liberals and Socialists, which themselves have come up through various extra-parliamentary mechanisms in the past.

Nonetheless, referendums clearly have a greater potential to break up old political alignments and alliances than ordinary elections. The resultant fluidity and confusion may well give the impression that this is a concomitant of popular participation. Owing to the parties' ability to determine when and on what subject a referendum will be held, in most of the countries we are considering, this impression is mistaken. The confusion and instability manifest in many (though not all) referendum campaigns derives from the issues they are held on rather than from the character of the popular consultation. That is to say, if government parties choose to hold referendums primarily on matters on which they themselves (and often their main opponents) are internally divided, naturally these dissensions will show themselves in the campaign. But they stem from the impact of the issue itself, not from the fact that it is the subject of a referendum. The divisions would manifest themselves wherever it was decided – in Parliament or in a general election if no referendum were held.

A pertinent current example is that of the divisions in the British Conservative Party (and, to a much lesser extent, in Labour) about developments in the relationship with the European Union. The party is strongly split: the previous leader Margaret Thatcher fell partly because of her hostility to 'Brussels'. Quarrels have intensified under her successor John Major, particularly after the General Election victory of 1992. Some members have been expelled for voting against the party on 'European' issues in Parliament. As a compromise, a referendum is increasingly promoted on whether Britain should join in a single European currency.

Now clearly such a referendum would oppose one wing of the Conservatives to another. Each would make common cause with allies in the other parties. Arguments would fly across the traditional divides. The distinctively pro-European Liberals could make a decisive breakthrough, profiting from the spectacle of prominent Conservatives at each others' throats. Yet all this would already have been prefigured in Parliament and in other party and electoral arenas and would intrude into the referendum rather than being precipitated by it.

Referendums do not seem inherently more divisive for parties than ordinary representative elections, therefore. What of their substantive results? Leaving aside the cases we shall consider in more detail in the following sections, the judgement of the most recent comprehensive review (Butler and Ranney, 1994, p. 263) is that, within their limits, 'the consequences of most referendums seem to have been beneficial'.

The qualifications on the statement relate in part to the control of official institutions over what is voted on, which as we have seen restricts referendums to two broad areas rather than covering the whole range of policy questions. Still, these are often questions which pose major political difficulties, so the ability of popular voting to come up with sensible and not obviously mistaken decisions testifies to electoral good sense and prudence.

Given the powers of government over the timing of the consultation and very often their ability to get more extensive and favourable treatment of their own proposals in the media, could we, however, regard the outcomes as due more to elite persuasion than inherent good sense on the part of electors? This would ignore the fact that the results often go against elite preferences, sometimes in a startling way. Striking examples cited by Butler and Ranney are the Norwegian and Swiss decisions against closer association with the EU, the New Zealand vote in favour of electoral reform, the Chilean vote of 1988 favouring democracy against the authoritarian regime, the Canadian rejection of the Meech Lake Accord on a new relationship between Quebec and the Federal Government. These decisions (however negative from the point of view of the elite) are far from blind protest voting. The alternatives actually endorsed have at least as much of a claim to be considered responsible and constructive as their opposites.

As Butler and Ranney observe, referendums are hardly direct democracy in action, because of the constraints upon them; and they do not clearly support either the extravagant hopes of their proponents or the exaggerated fears of their critics. They see them nonetheless as making a modest contribution to opening up the policy process and helping to resolve some crisis that might not have been settled by other means, and to that extent their judgement of them is positive. More recourse to referendums along the same lines is not going to destabilize the polity but may help it with some political problems.

4.3 The Working of Direct Initiatives: The American States

This is a far cry, however, from endorsing full popular participation along the lines urged by Barber (1984) or Pateman (1970). Nor can one easily extend the lessons from selective, infrequent, carefully regulated referendums to the continuing electronic consultation envisaged under the party-based model of direct democracy of chapter 2.

A slightly closer approximation, though far from an exact match, is found in the experience of some American States with the policy initiative. The initiative, unlike a referendum, can be called on any question by any group in the population which collects enough signatures. (There are varying rules about what quantity is required but it is generally enough to ensure that the proposal has serious backing, so that it is not purely frivolous.)

This transfer of the power to initiate from legislature to population clearly extends the range of topics and the possible occasions on which consultations may be held. It thus gives more opportunity to examine the impact of popular interventions and the consequences they produce than in the case of the more severely constrained referendums. We accordingly devote this section to examining what has happened in the twenty or so American States which use some kind of initiative, before going on to examine the experiences of Switzerland and Italy in the following two sections.

Unlike the European examples, the provisions for popular consultation in the American States were part of a package of reforms, inspired by the Progressive movement at the beginning of the century, to weaken and undermine the influence of political parties. Along with provisions for direct popular voting on legislation, these included the substitution of primary elections for party caucuses to select candidates, the elimination of corruption and party patronage, institution of non-partisan elections for many local offices, and recall of elected officials on popular petitions. Together with pre-existing features such as the separation of legislative and executive powers and provisions for judicial review, and reinforced by social changes such as the extension of health and other insurance provisions and enhanced medical care (which reduced the need for party handouts), these measures have weakened party organization and reduced parties' ability to function as policy co-ordinators across the different institutional levels of State politics.

Commentators agree, however, that the provisions for popular consultation played a minor part in this process compared to the measures directly affecting parties or even to concurrent social changes (Cronin, 1989, p. 224). Anti-party attitudes did, however, induce parties to leave the initiating and debating of direct legislation to other groups. This was in spite of the fact that party loyalty and affiliations are one of the major ways voters link stands on initiatives to their own interests and policy-preferences (Cronin, 1989, p. 70; Magleby 1984, pp. 174–9).

As a proportion of overall legislation in each State, popular initiatives never exceed 10 per cent and are often much less. Hence, the vast bulk of legislation is still passed by parties and representatives in the legislature. This contributes to the aloofness of parties from direct legislation, for the same reasons as those discussed previously in regard to referendums: as initiatives are held on a small minority of issues which are often ones deliberately avoided by parties anyway because of their potential for stirring up internal divisions, leaders can avoid internal problems by deliberately not taking a stand. This is particularly the case when the issues involved are not central to their legislative programme, which is in any case less closely articulated at State than at Federal level.

In a few cases where an issue might centrally affect the parties, on the other hand, as with anti-tax proposals in Michigan and several other States about 1984, a coalition centred around parties was formed to defend tax-supported services (Cronin, 1989, pp. 205–6).

Direct legislation, therefore, while it may restrict party activity to some extent, still leaves parties able to intervene where essential interests are threatened. It also leaves the vast bulk of business in their hands to be dealt with by the normal legislative process.

Initiatives moreover tend to concentrate on the same areas as the referendums discussed in the preceding section. There is relatively heavy coverage of the moral and environmental areas, some constitutional and rights questions (including matters affecting minorities), and fiscal matters. Yet other areas, arguably more important and central both to party and electors' concerns, get left out. Thus issues like employment and general economic management are rarely or never the subject of initiatives, even though they affect more people more directly than the questions which get voted on (Magleby, 1994a, p. 238, table 7.3).

That this is the case is due to another feature of American initiatives. Owing to the Progressives' eagerness to displace political parties, popular consultation was conceived as a legislative process designed to complement or replace representative voting with the will of the sovereign people. As a result, initiatives often are presented as draft legislation. An incidental result of this is to limit understanding of their general import and effect. The quasi-legal form they take also renders them instruments better adapted to affect policy in some areas, traditionally controlled by legislation, than in others of greater importance which are 'managed' by government. The obvious example is employment, where one cannot legislate directly for a fall in the numbers unemployed. A more flexible formulation of initiatives might allow for endorsement of policy priorities which would more directly affect areas of central concern to electors.

A further consequence of the legislative strait-jacket on the formulation of initiatives, and of party aloofness, is the lack of information electors have about them. Most States prepare a pamphlet covering what may be a lengthy list of initiatives on any one ballot, usually with a summary of the content, a list of arguments pro and con, and a short title. Even this may make difficult reading, however, and substantial numbers of electors fail to look at the pamphlet. A standard reaction of electorates on complicated, technical and difficult bills is to vote for the status quo. This is one reason why an average of only 36 per cent of initiatives are formally passed (Magleby, 1994b, p. 93).

The difficulty of understanding what many initiatives are getting at also accounts for a 'drop-off' among electors voting for candidates for office, to those also voting for initiatives. This is of the order of 10–15 per cent. Typically the people who fail to vote on initiatives are the less educated and less politically involved elements in the population. To that extent those who vote on policy are better informed and educated than those who vote in representative elections.

As one might expect, the more important and controversial measures attract more attention and stimulate higher turnout. These are also the issues where parties are more likely to get involved, if only indirectly, and where political ideology enables electors to relate their vote to other preferences and interests, as the competing alternatives and their implications are better clarified (Magleby, 1994b, p. 95).

The general lack of party involvement with popular initiatives clearly leaves the field open to other groups who may have a political axe to grind, predominantly special interests of one kind or another. This can be seen as a negative development for two reasons. In the first place, interest groups, however public-spirited their aims, appeal only to one segment of public opinion. They have no particular motivation to balance and if possible resolve competing interests, as political parties with a broad-based support coalition might have. Moreover, the situation of campaigning for a particular measure puts a premium on confrontation and conflict with opposing forces rather than the typical kind of policy-bargaining in which parties engage within a representative assembly (Magleby, 1984, p. 188).

In the second place the predominance of interest groups raises worries that businesses and others financially affected by decisions may gain disproportionate influence on the process. This worry is reinforced by the growth of an 'initiative industry' of public relations consultants and advisers, which will collect the necessary signatures for any desired initiative, advise on framing the proposition, and then campaign for it. While in theory any group could draw on this 'industry', in practice it is business which will have most resources and most need to rely on it.

All this might seem to add up to a predominance of producer-orientated and generally conservative groups in initiative campaigns. Surprisingly, this does not seem to be the case – not at any rate without major qualifications (Magleby, 1984, p. 141; Cronin, 1989, pp. 99–116).

Major anti-gun legislation was supported against extensively financed opposition in several Eastern States and the same was true of anti-nuclear provisions in the West. Tax limitation initiatives were passed in several States at the end of the 1970s under the influence of the Californian Proposition 13, but tax-upholding initiatives else-where won when the general economic situation became tighter and services needed to be maintained.

The main influence of well-financed business-sponsored campaigns is exerted in defeating initiatives rather than passing them. This veto power is linked to the tendency of electors to support the status quo anyway when they are doubtful about the implications of the legislation. A negative campaign aimed at generating doubt obviously plays on this tendency. Yet business interests' money can be balanced by groups which generate enough enthusiasm to get volunteers lobbying for them and to raise the profile of the issue enough for both pros and cons to be widely debated. Enthusiasm as well as money attracts media coverage, which can in turn neutralize the advantages of the better-financed side.

Many of these aspects of initiative campaigns are not too dissimilar from points made elsewhere in the literature about campaigning for office in the American States – with the crucial difference where candidates are involved that they generally have a party label and are thus tied to a particular legislative record and general programme. Where there is no differential party labelling, as in primary elections in one-party-predominant States, electors are equally at a loss in regard to candidates (Greenstein, 1970, pp. 39, 67; Cronin, 1989, p. 78).

Voting on policy in American States may not be noticeably less informed or in general inferior to the quality of the electoral choice involved in the selection of representatives at the same level. But it clearly does not live up to the expectations of its advocates that it would stimulate voters' interest and enthusiasm, bring a breath of fresh popular air into the foetid party-dominated corridors of power, and materially change politics in the States where it was introduced. Judging it against these ideals Magleby (1984, pp. 192–9) found it distinctly wanting, though in a later judgement (1994a, pp. 254–7) he sees some positive merits in the opportunities it offers to get fresh issues on the agenda.

In both appraisals, Magleby identifies the greatest defect of direct legislation in US States as bypassing and weakening the political parties, which constitute the best means of clarifying and balancing the political debate. Cronin, in an assessment at the end of the 1980s, concurs on this weakness of direct legislation and indeed sees greater party involvement in it as a major way of remedying informational and other weaknesses (1989, pp. 70, 230).

Cronin's evaluation of the achievements of direct legislation also raises the important question of outcomes rather than simply the 'process characteristics' of initiatives and popular referendums. Has direct legislation had any of the negative effects which those distrustful of populism have feared – threats to minority rights, overweening use of majority powers, preference for left-wing over right-wing positions or vice versa, covert predominance of business interests, inconsistency and instability of policies?

Cronin's judgement on all these is basically favourable. In none of these aspects does direct legislation seem notably inferior or even wildly different from the measures passed by State legislatures in the same period (Cronin, 1989, pp. 196–219). It has merits in raising matters which get ignored by parties and legislatures, stimulating them to think ahead to issues which might get popular attention, and in general increasing their responsiveness and attention to the public. These modest merits are far from the great expectations conceived by their original proponents but they are real and significant enough to justify the retention of direct legislation as a feature of the State constitutions which have it, and even to view with equanimity the spread of the practice elsewhere (Cronin, 1989, pp. 250–1). This view echoes that of Butler and Ranney in their review of referendums in the world at large (1994, p. 263).

4.4 Popular Policy-votes in Switzerland

More than half the popular consultations ever held at national level in the world have taken place in Switzerland (Butler and Ranney, 1994, p. 5). This does not include consultations held at Cantonal level (Switzerland has twenty-six cantons and half-cantons corresponding broadly to US States) or even at the level of communes within cantons, which have considerable autonomy. Some smaller German-speaking cantons are indeed full direct democracies with a popular assembly substituting for Parliament. In some others, all parliamentary Acts are voted upon by the populace.

In a typical year during the last two decades Swiss citizens might thus have had to vote on up to sixteen Federal consultations and double or triple that number at the State and local level (Knüsel and Hottinger, 1994, pp. 32–3). Federal consultations are often grouped, so citizens may vote on four together three or four times a year.

Swiss Federal consultations include obligatory ones required to ratify foreign treaties, and popular initiatives for constitutional change. No initiative is provided for at the ordinary legislative level, (Linder 1994, p. 90) but the distinction is blurred because similar policy proposals can be made as in the American States under the guise of a constitutional amendment to Federal competences. Thus, in practice, an extensive power of popular initiative is exercised which has the same coverage as in the United States (Kriesi, 1994, p. 72, table 3; Magleby, 1994a, p. 238, table 7.3).

Besides privileging the rights of individual citizens at Federal level, Swiss democracy also privileges Federalism. There must be concurrent majorities in a majority of cantons for proposals to pass, thus in principle giving a right of veto to the 25 per cent of the population living in smaller cantons (Linder, 1994, p. 74). Even so, popular majorities have had a determining effect on measures of the highest importance, including Switzerland's accession to the European Economic Area (50.3 per cent against) and in the canton of Graubünden in imposing restrictions on road transport. These have major consequences for most other European countries, given that three major Alpine passes run through the area.

Despite their importance, popular consultations do not always attract a high turnout. Participation in fact varies between the 30 per cent of electors who always vote to around 70 per cent for bills of

greater general interest which attract sporadic voters. Around 20 per
cent of electors never vote on single issues (Linder 1994, p. 94). As in
the American States, turnout varies with the importance of the issue,
economic/constitutional questions like accession to the European
Economic Area attracting highest interest.

In terms of substantive outcomes there is a high rate of support for
the status quo. Where constitutional amendments are proposed by
the Federal Assembly as obligatory referendums, roughly two-thirds
pass. The success rate of government-sponsored measures in general
is 63.3 per cent (Kobach, 1994, p. 130, table 4.2). The success rate for
popular initiatives is only 10 per cent (Linder, 1994, p. 99) compared
to 36 per cent in the American States (Magleby, 1984a, p. 93). The
same difference with the success rates (61 per cent) of Parliamentary
sponsored initiatives appears in the US. However, this underestimates
the influence of the Swiss initiatives since Federal politicians often
compromise by anticipating them in Parliamentary bills or by producing counter-proposals which concede some of the points at issue – a
phenomenon which has also been noted for the American States
(Magleby, 1994a, p. 253).

Linder (1994, p. 145) notes as a difference between Swiss and US
direct legislation, however, that it is not as important an influence on
power-sharing in the latter case. Minorities in Switzerland have been
better able than American blacks, for example, to use initiatives and
other devices to get their concerns on to the political agenda.

Other differences are that direct democracy is more central to the
whole Swiss political process than in the case of the US States, where
it is complementary and marginal and of course is used at the Federal
as well as State level. Despite this, there are remarkable similarities
between the process in both countries:

1   Government responsiveness is enhanced.

2   Nevertheless about 90 per cent of legislation is still carried
through by normal Parliamentary means and is not challenged.

3   Participation in direct legislation is patchy, does not generally
match up to the level in representative elections and favours the more
educated and prosperous.

4   Perhaps as a result, 'direct legislation does not produce unsound legislation or unwise or bad policy' (Linder, 1994, p. 143).
This is despite empirical evidence showing that citizens are relatively
poorly informed about the issues on which they vote (as they are of
course about candidates in legislative elections). Most of the time they
reject measures that would diminish rights, liberties and freedoms for

the less well-represented or less organized segments of society (Cronin, 1989, p. 123; Linder, 1994, p. 143). The so-called xenophobic initiatives of the 1970s and 1980s, restricting or expelling foreigners and immigrants, have been rejected by convincing popular majorities in Switzerland.

5   A further similarity noted by Linder is that 'direct democracy can influence the political agenda in favour of issues important to less well organized interests, (1994, p. 143). This has been very relevant for environmentalists, women and the poor in Switzerland (the social security system was built from the bottom up, starting with cantonal initiatives). Initiatives were also important historically to the Catholic and Socialist minorities in getting concessions and establishing themselves as important components of the Federal political process (Kriesi, 1994, p. 65).

6   Despite this, better-financed interests will, other things being equal, win campaigns for referendums and initiatives. This is particularly true where the issue is not of general interest, where voters do not have other guidance (as from parties or ideology) and where the proposal is complex. The influence of money is linked to the professionalization of campaign management, as the better-financed side can buy more expertise (Kriesi, 1994, pp. 73–84).

7   Linder's final conclusion is that direct democracy tends to strengthen single-issue and interest groups rather than political parties with larger, general-interest programmes (p. 144). This assessment is supported by Möckli (1994, p. 57) and Knüsel and Hottinger (1994, pp. 24–5). These latter all concur with the assessment of Kobach (1994, p. 132) that

> direct democracy has contributed greatly to the relative weakness of political parties in Switzerland. It has rendered redundant an otherwise important party function, the aggregation and articulation of political preferences in the electorate, by allowing citizens to express their opinions directly. At the same time, the initiative has undermined the parties' control of the national agenda. Referendums and initiatives have also weakened Swiss parties directly by undermining their unity. Ballot issues divide party membership on question after question, providing voters with repeated opportunities to defect from their party's position. With most referendums, ad hoc alliances of interest groups, parties, other organizations, and public figures spring up on both sides of the issue. Individual voters cannot be prevented from pursuing their own preferences. Parties can do little more than endorse a position and hope that the declaration sways enough voters. Quite often, voters ignore this advice. Survey data over the 1977–80 period showed that, on average, 51 per cent of FDP supporters knowingly voted against the

recommendations of their party, as did 55 per cent of Christian Democrats and 60 per cent of Social Democrats. Fully 75 per cent of the supporters of the agrarian Swiss People's party disregarded their party's recommendations.

One should, however, note that Linder (1994, p. 112) dissents from this last point, saying that electors follow the party position when they know it and when it is consistent with its general ideological stance.

Kobach attributes defections on the part of electors to the fact that party endorsements of particular positions do not appear on the ballot paper, so electors lack guidance on how to cast their vote. We have already noted the importance of this simple but fundamental absence of party guidance in the case of American States. However, at elite level too Swiss parties often diverge internally on specific issues. Party colleagues may endorse opposing sides on the same issue, as in 1986 on whether Switzerland should join the UN, when the presidents of the opposing committees were both members of the Radicals (FDP).

Kobach notes that, paradoxically, the governmental position of Swiss political parties is not weakened by this situation. They have long commanded steadfast voting loyalty in general elections. It is against this background that a different assessment of the consequences of direct legislation for the political parties is made by Kriesi (1994, pp. 68–73). Far from seeing parties as disunited by referendums and initiatives, he identifies them as the major sponsors and promoters of 49 per cent of the former and about three-quarters of the latter. Furthermore, he sees different kinds of consultation as favouring different kinds of party – the referendums usually allowing conservative parties to defend the status quo on the basis of popular votes, although recently the left has used it to block right-wing motions for change. The initiative on the other hand favours the left unambiguously, though as we have seen its success rate is not high (but it may have indirect effects). Kobach concurs on this point insofar as he sees the smaller non-governmental parties uniting on initiatives to oppose the governmental parties' position (1994, pp. 133–4).

Kriesi's point about the way in which direct policy proposals may strengthen rather than weaken party positions is supported by long-term historical analysis. Linder offers a summary which to a considerable extent goes against his own conclusions on the weakening effect of popular consultations on parties (1994, pp. 19–21, 29–31). The modern, more tightly centralized Swiss Federation was imposed by the Radical party after it won a civil war in 1848 against the conservative Catholics (40 per cent of the population). These were excluded from Federal power and to some extent discriminated against until the introduction of referendums in 1874 enabled them to impose a systematic block on Federal action through popular vote. The Radicals were then forced to take the Catholic political party into government and accept proportional representation at the end of the First World War. The same thing happened with the Social Democrats from 1918 to 1959, when they finally became permanent partners with the bourgeois parties in the unchanging Federal government coalition. (Kobach, 1994, p. 102, concurs with this point.)

Coalition politics at governmental level in fact, rather than voting on single issues by the electors, explains many of the peculiarities of Swiss politics and policy-making. Parties in all coalitions, and particularly in permanent ones, have to compromise with their partners – who may as in Switzerland be of a very different ideological tradition. In turn, this imposes internal strains between party compromisers and ideological purists. Thus on many questions there may be internal minorities and majorities, but this is as, or more, likely to be between those disposed to find a compromise with their government partners and those who wish to stick it out, as between two groups taking different sides for the referendum. The history of German, French, Austrian, Dutch and Belgian coalitions – countries with few or no popular referendums – demonstrates this. Even single-party governments and oppositions divide over issues without the pressures of direct voting, as the experiences of the British Labour Party and the Social Democrats in the 1980s, and of the Eurosceptics and Europhiles in the Conservative Party of the 1990s, clearly demonstrate.

One of the points at issue between Kriesi and the opposing Swiss commentators may in fact be on the definition of a party division. Majority endorsement of a position by a party may be taken as evidence of a split or accepted as a normal state of affairs within the party. Assessments are often coloured by the vision of a totally united, ideologically pure party – which has rarely if ever existed in practice. As we shall see below, Uleri's (1994b, pp. 411–14) assessment of Italian initiatives identifies stands taken by the parties where others have seen them as disunited (Bogdanor, 1994, pp. 65–6). A comparison with Italian Parliamentary legislation would, however, show the parties as always disunited. So one either discounts their ability ever to take a policy stand on anything, or identifies the party position with that of the dominant faction, as Uleri does on popular initiatives. Such an assessment seems realistic, as the official party position on both policy and coalition negotiations *is* that of the dominant faction.

Although Swiss coalitions seem to differentiate the situation there from that of the United States, in fact the separation of powers between two legislative houses and an executive Governorship means that policy coalitions have to be formed at every turn in State politics to get Parliamentary policies and legislation through. This is lauded both by Magleby (1984, pp. 188–90) and by Cronin (1989, p. 248) as creating a need for compromise and pragmatism which does not exist at popular level. In making assessments of party functioning, however, one cannot have one's cake and eat it. If cross-party coalitions and internal division are a good thing at Parliamentary level, they must be a good thing at popular level too.

Clearly one can also see legislative policy coalitions as weakening parties, however. Surely, given the marginality of popular consultations in most States, the Parliamentary effect is greater than that of initiatives. Indeed, the weakening of popular majorities was foreseen and planned for by the founders of the US constitution (Madison, 1787–8/1911) on which State practices have been modelled.

In seeking reasons for the weakness of American parties (if they really *are* weak – we shall consider this in chapter 5) it seems fairer to look for explanations in State constitutions as a whole, rather than isolating the popular initiative for blame. Similarly the permanent Swiss coalition seems as or more likely to affect the parties composing it as does direct popular legislation.

A last point from the Swiss experience is that popular consultation leads to compromise and power-sharing rather than conflict. This is in contrast to the view of Magleby (1984, p. 184), for example, that direct legislation intensifies conflict. Perhaps in reality it does both. By allowing problems bypassed by most politicians to be considered it does indeed raise political stakes for the moment. But by discussing and, hopefully, resolving them rather than letting them fester, it contributes to long-term stability. Certainly initiatives and referendums seem to produce authoritative resolutions of key problems (Ranney, 1994b, p. 34). Possibly for this reason their continuation and extension are supported by 80 per cent of the population in both the American States and Switzerland (Cronin, 1989, pp. 79–80; Linder, 1994, p. 134).

4.5 Popular Initiatives in Italy 1970–1994

Although constitutional referendums, including ones involving territorial questions, had been held in Italy before, a special form of popular initiative to abrogate existing legislation was introduced in the early 1970s. As Uleri (1994a and b) emphasizes, both the introduction of this procedure and its use have been powered by the political parties. The form of the initiative is negative – to express opposition to divorce, for example, one has to vote 'yes' for a proposal to abolish the existing law permitting divorce. This contorted procedure has been a feature of both Swiss and American State initiatives, which has been blamed for mistaken voting in the American case (Magleby, 1984, pp. 134, 144; Cronin, 1989, p. 74). The active participation of parties in Italy, however, helps inform electors about the way to express their real preferences, so the negative form of the ballot does not emerge as a problem there.

Abolition of a law gives a signal that new legislation is required, and the outcome also gives a clear indication of what it should be. Thus, although Parliament actually effects the new legislation, in all but one case (the civil liability of magistrates in 1987) it has followed the expression of majority opinion in doing so. The Constitutional Court plays a stronger role than is usual in the Swiss and American cases, and has disallowed some results of environmental initiatives on grounds of insufficient participation. It also has the power to decide if a proposal is suitable for popular vote in the first place and has exercised this power of review quite strongly. (One-third of requests supported by requisite signatures have been rejected – Uleri, 1994b, table 2.)

The negative form taken by the abrogative initiative is also misleading if a rejection is taken merely as indicating support for the status quo. Up to 1985 all initiatives were rejected (38 per cent of all initiatives from 1970 to 1993). However, many of these proposed the abolition of radical reform legislation, particularly in social matters. On the whole, initiatives in Italy have resulted in support for change – in society, economy and political procedures. This contrasts with the bias in favour of the status quo shown elsewhere, but may reflect the perceived need for change in Italy, where minority vetoes inside Parliament and government have prevented much needed modernization.

As elsewhere, the threat or approach of initiatives may induce governing parties to pass legislation in advance which concedes or compromises the point at issue. Initiatives thus have an important long-term effect in putting matters on the agenda, or breaking a legislative stalemate, which goes beyond their immediate outcome.

Points of similarity between Italian direct legislation and the Swiss and American experiences are thus that government responsiveness is enhanced, even though the vast bulk of policy measures are the exclusive concern of parliament. The actual decisions made have not been unsound or imprudent and indeed have often been rendered necessary by the inability of parliament or government to act. They have not threatened minorities and have been relatively neutral as between left-wing and right-wing positions. The majority is also capable of looking beyond its immediate interests; for example, an initiative promoted by the PCI (Communists) to maintain the cost-of-living increase for workers, regarded as economically untenable by the government parties, was rejected by the majority who would have benefited. Clearly Italian initiatives have also helped 'new' groups and parties (environmentalists and women in particular) to get their issues on the agenda.

The differences between Italy and the other political systems using popular initiatives are, however, very important, particularly as they may be traced to the involvement of political parties in the process of direct legislation. Nobody has claimed that voting in initiatives in Italy is less informed than voting in elections. This is probably because the parties (or at least their dominant factions) both debate the issues and give clear indications of what side they are on (see Uleri, 1994a, 412–15, table 3, for a list of party positions on each initiative). Participation is lower than in general elections but still very high, averaging around 75 per cent of electors for most consultations.

Following from this, it is not the case that better-financed or organized interests win. The Catholic 'movimento per la vita', backed by the Church and allied conservatives, lost initiatives on divorce and abortion to the much less well-financed and organized secular groups. Environmentalists won votes against hunters in 1990, although the latter succeeded in keeping participation down to under 50 per cent, inducing the Constitutional Court to disallow the result. There is no 'signature industry' – again because political parties substitute.

Underlying all these differences is the fact of party involvement in the initiative campaigns. The new Radical Party was the prime mover of most of the initiatives in the 1970s and early 1980s, and was again prominent in prompting electoral reforms in the early 1990s. This corresponds to the use by the Swiss non-governmental parties of initiatives to promote themselves. However, the established Italian parties took to promoting initiatives in the mid-1980s and consistently took a position on them consonant with that they took on Parliamentary legislation.

At both levels, parties were internally divided. This was a fact of life for Italian parties in the post-war period, when factions in all of them, with the partial exception of the Communists, had well-defined 'correnti' with an established position, recognized leader, and sometimes separate organizations. Parties often divided on Parliamentary voting, so it is no surprise if this happened also in the course of popular consultations.

Nevertheless the controlling faction was decisive in deciding, for example, when parties would enter or leave governmental coalitions, and where the majority of its votes would go in Parliamentary divisions. Similarly, it defined the official position in referendums and initiatives, thus giving a lead which its electors could follow. This does not sound too different from the Swiss situation described by Kobach (1994, pp. 132–3). The difference is that Kobach is contrasting the messy world of real-life popular campaigning with the ideal of a disciplined, ideologically coherent, united party. Uleri on the other hand is comparing party stands on initiatives with party stands in parliament, and finding little difference in terms of party division and factionalization at each level. The party was still able to make official recommendations, and this seems to have counted with its electors.

By the 1990s, however, the old parties of the Centre and Right were in crisis. Was this a result of their involvement in initiatives? These certainly helped promote changes in the electoral and hence the party sphere by approving measures for a constituency-based first-past-the-post system for electing MPs. Moreover, the initiatives were supported by coalitions of politicians from different parties, corresponding quite closely to the Swiss situation as described by Kobach.

However, the reason why established parties were not important actors in the Italian initiatives of the 1990s was that they were already falling apart under judicial investigation of massive corruption and links with organized crime. These had nothing to do with the Italian approximation to direct democracy and everything to do with the established parties' desire to hang on to government power and dispense patronage. The general weakness of Italian parties was exacerbated by a parliamentary situation which made wheeling and dealing central to governing. In this context the use of the popular initiative probably helped to strengthen rather than weaken the system by enabling it to produce some authoritative and popular measures. Initiatives helped smooth the peaceful transition from the 'First' to the 'Second' Republic, by producing authoritative decisions about a new electoral system (Uleri, 1994b, p. 427).

4.6 Conclusions

Chapter 5 will systematically relate these analyses of the existing processes and consequences of direct legislation to our concern with direct democracy. This will help answer unresolved questions about how citizens and parties would actually function in such a system. As stressed from the outset, however, we cannot straightforwardly use the evidence from current initatives and referendums to say how people would behave in an electronically based direct democracy. Representative parliaments in all existing systems (except for some small Swiss cantons) continue to make the bulk of individual decisions. Direct legislation is often passed under peculiar institutional forms which affect outcomes. So we have to interpret and extrapolate from our evidence rather than apply it directly to decide whether a full-blown direct democracy is viable.

Nevertheless, the analyses cited here do provide us with a basis for factual evaluation which can usefully complement the theoretical analysis undertaken in chapter 3. Of particular interest is the fact that citizens and politicians in different countries react in similar ways to the opportunities and costs involved in direct voting. This gives us a useful opening to generalize about its likely effects across different social and cultural contexts, as we now proceed to do.

5

Citizens and Parties under Direct Democracy

5.1 Introduction

In this chapter we focus particularly on two questions which loom large in our previous discussion. The first is whether citizens are equal to the task of making direct policy choices, in terms of their inherent capacities and the objective constraints upon them. There are the types of arguments and counter-arguments typically grouped under (4) – capacity – in table 3.1, but which spill over into the others grouped under (3) – does mass involvement typically lead to majority tyranny? – and (5) – the lack of balancing forces in direct democracy to counteract the likely deficiencies of citizens. The last two groupings of arguments also involve the functioning and indeed the survival of the political parties. This is the second question we focus upon here (the last two sections of this chapter).

The reason for our concern with parties will be obvious and emerges centrally from the arguments of chapters 2 and 3. That is, that they are crucial in forming and organizing public opinion and transmitting it into government action. This is probably true of all political entities but above all for mass democracies.

Without some organizations to define and defend proposals the analysis of chapter 4 shows that most opinion will remain inchoate and electors will probably tend to vote for the status quo. Single-issue organizations focused on the policy at stake may be useful in drawing attention to previously ignored problems, and in rousing enthusiasm for some political action. This is important for any kind of democracy. They are inclined to push their point of view without regard to other considerations, however. Parties on the other hand, operating across a range of issues and having to put them together for government, are always under some pressure to seek balance and compatibility, even if they can often go overboard on single issues too.

Parties have the other advantage that their operations are public and they are known quantities, tied to a particular record and ideology. As we have seen, interest groups often intervene on single issues, sometimes through front organizations, in matters where they have a financial stake. Party participation diminishes the possibility of hidden manipulation as it brings this kind of involvement into the open.

Similar advantages stem from the participation of parties in elections under representative democracy (section 2.3). Where there is party affiliation, electors can link candidates to a known record rather than electing individuals whose views on most matters are unknown, and thus make informed choices – just as they can with policies under direct democracy. The stark alternative of direct versus representative democracy may thus be substantially less important than the question of whether both are based on parties, which tie in single issues and candidates to a general, known, position.

What, though, if direct democracy corrodes the very basis on which parties stand? – that is, their organizational support, electoral loyalty, control of government and ideological coherence? That would, in light of what I have just said, be a very powerful argument against moving from representative to direct democracy. What we need to do therefore is to examine this objection on as factual a basis as we can manage with the evidence we have reviewed. Some commentators detect a weakening of parties under direct legislation while others disagree. We have to reach some overall judgement on what is actually happening in the cases examined and apply this to direct democracy generally.

These discussions about parties are not independent of the ones we shall consider first, on the capacity of citizens. For clearly this is not purely a matter of individual characteristics. The better-educated may be able to make more sense of confusing information and to cast their vote strategically but the evidence indicates that they are often unnecessarily confused by institutional constraints and complexities. Parties stand out as one of the mediating institutions that may enhance electoral understanding and competence.

We shall consider parties in this light in section 5.3, where we examine technological and institutional innovations which may enhance the quality of direct voting. First we shall look at what the empirical studies allow us to infer about individual citizen capacities, overall outcomes and balance and the possibility of popular tyranny.

We go on to consider these in the next section. Before doing so, however, we should note that the traditionally most important objection to mass democracy, its sheer technical impossibility, is for the final time laid to rest by these studies. Even with physical collection and distribution of ballot papers, and print technology of the nineteenth century, mass voting on policy and some debate can and does take place. What actually happens in American States, Switzerland and Italy (and in terms of referendums, many other countries of the world) is clearly feasible elsewhere. One hopes it can be improved on and this is one element in our discussion below. Opposition to direct legislation must, however, be seen as based not on its infeasibility, but either on a general aversion to power-sharing or on the set of philosophical arguments and factual assertions considered in chapter 3. What I hope to do here is to apply – particularly to the factual assertions about how direct democracy would function – the kind of serious discussion which, given the slow but steady spread of popular participation in the world today, they clearly deserve.

5.2 Public Capability

One set of arguments with a respectable ancestry is whether ordinary people are up to the effort of debating and deciding all important policies. Such objections range from doubts about how much information they are capable of collecting and assimilating, or how far they can actually use it to make informed decisions, to the amount of time they could or would want to spend on deciding. Pessimistic conclusions on these individual capacities of the citizen then lead to negative expectations about how they would behave in the mass, from being hoodwinked by demagogues and covert interests to passing contradictory policies with scant consideration for minorities diverging from the views or social composition of the current majority.

Doubts about citizens' capacity thus extend from the micro-level of their individual characteristics to the macro-consequences of policy-making by ill-informed majorities. Departing from the usual sequence of discussion, we shall consider mass collective behaviour, outcomes and macro-level consequences first and then go on to consider individuals. After all, if direct democracy manages to overcome the defective qualities of individuals or even to combine them in such a way as to arrive at good public decisions in spite of them, it would have even more to commend it than if it depended solely on good individual qualities to succeed.

An obvious analogy here is the free market, which is widely praised for taking each individual's purely selfish choices and aggregating them in such a way as to serve the collective good. So are 'economic' theories of (representative) democracy, which show how selfish and short-sighted politicians, and citizens blind to any conception of the public interest, can interact to produce the public decision best calculated to please most people and meet their central demands (Downs, 1957).

At the macro-level therefore it may be a positive virtue for a system to be able to operate optimally even with the worst imaginable support base. Critiques of the individual capacity of citizens may thus be beside the point provided the overall system operates well. What then does the evidence show us?

There is no doubt but that it presents direct democracy in a very positive light. Most commentators (Cronin, 1989, pp. 229–32; Linder, 1994, p. 143; Uleri, 1994b, pp. 422–7 – but see Magleby, 1984, pp. 190–8 for a generally negative assessment) agree on the generally beneficial or at least balanced nature of decisions taken by popular consultation. In making this evaluation they use the central criteria which enter into the debate over direct democracy, such as the consistency and coherence of public policy and tolerance of minority rights. There is absolutely no sign of a majority steamroller imposing its views on everyone else. Far from it. There is a general predisposition to keep the status quo, especially where the consequences of action are unclear. While that might be thought to favour the Right ideologically, we have seen (especially where environmental disturbance is concerned) that it may also advantage the Left. Enough radical and progressive measures have in any case been passed to invalidate the idea that popular voting produces easily predictable outcomes favouring one ideological tendency over another.

It is of course notoriously hard to say what is a 'good' political decision as opposed to a 'bad'. Judgements have tended to be coloured by commentators' own ideological sympathies. Is the Swiss referendum deciding (by a slim majority) against further association with the European Union a choice which will bring positive or negative consequences in the long term? The elites think it will be negative but of course it can be argued that Switzerland's strategic position gives the country an economic stranglehold over its neighbours anyway, so it may have all the benefits and incur no costs by holding aloof.

In the Italian case there is agreement that popular initiatives unblocked and validated necessary decisions which the parliament could not make on its own. In the case of the American States many individual results of individual initiatives (tax limitations, gun laws, harsh criminal penalties) can be satirized. However, there are always counter-examples where initiatives have supported public services against tax cuts, limited guns, upheld minority rights and protected the environment. Given the difficulty of saying what is 'objectively' good or bad, perhaps the safest ground for evaluation is to compare popular initiatives with what State legislatures have done. Here very little difference opens up. Parallels can be found for all the decisions taken by initiatives in those taken by State legislators without popular consultation (Cronin, 1989, pp. 73, 229; Magleby does not make this comparison).

If outcomes are much the same in both cases, the argument can of course be reversed. What is the point of imposing the burdens of decision-making on citizens when representatives will make similar decisions anyway? This, however, loses sight of the overwhelming democratic need for consent. As argued in chapter 1, all types of democracy rest so much on popular consent and participation that the need to maximize them is always evident. Wherever possible, consent must be obtained, if democracy is to be true to itself. This is not in dispute.

The only way therefore that defenders of representative as against direct forms can justify limiting popular endorsements of decisions is by pointing to the dangers and inconveniences that these carry with them. Among the most important are the bad decisions that would be taken by the masses – bad in terms of not effectively tackling problems and bad also by democratic standards of protecting minorities, preserving coherence, consistency etc.

It need only be demonstrated therefore that direct legislation does not lead to these consequences (and certainly no more than parliamentary measures) for this case in terms of the negative consequences of participation to collapse. If it has no negative consequences, the democratic need to base itself on the highest possible levels of participation and consent is so overwhelming that it pushes us in the direction of direct democracy of its own weight, the impediments being shown not to exist.

This is perhaps a strong statement but it is justified by the fact that these outcomes have emerged, in the case of the American States at least, from the very situation that might have been expected to produce the opposite – that is, direct popular unmediated voting. Most American State initiatives, as we have noted, are carried through without the participation of political parties, for various reasons. This causes discussion and voting on them to resemble nothing more than the unmediated form of direct democracy described, and criticized for its susceptibility to ill-considered decisions, in chapter 2. If, in spite of an institutional set-up almost designed to produce policy incoherence, rash judgements and majority tyranny, the outcomes which emerge are reasonably prudent and balanced, this must surely demonstrate that popular voting on policy is less to be feared than its critics have suggested.

This is a very powerful point and bears expanding and repeating. It is perhaps no wonder that the policies coming out of Swiss and Italian initiatives are beneficial or at least not objectionable, given that parties give a lead and (in Italy at any rate) are reasonably successful in mobilizing voters round their point of view. Commentators agree that the quality of voters' information would also be much enhanced in the American States if parties intervened more. Mistakes would be avoided and there would be a much clearer tie-in between particular decisions and overall policies.

This is not in doubt and more extensive party participation in direct democracy is one of the major forms of institutional improvement which we consider in the next section. But even without the moderating effects of party guidance the fact remains that US State voters have on balance taken good and prudent decisions on policy.

Two reflections follow from this. One is, how much better they would do if the institutional and technological context within which they take these decisions were improved – allowing for a more flexible and continuously available information flow, for example, as well as party guidance. The second is that, since moderate mediating institutions (as opposed to interested and often covert and manipulative pressure groups) are absent in initiatives, the generally positive consequences of these must derive from citizens' own qualities of character. This further reinforces the case for moving to direct democracy, since it argues that ordinary citizens can be trusted to act responsibly. We now consider their qualifications for doing so.

The major criticisms usually made of electors' ability to decide on policy is of the limited information they have or can acquire on the consequences of the policy they are voting on, and their inability to assimilate and use the information to make an informed decision (Sartori, 1987, pp. 115–20; Magleby, 1984, pp. 197–8). A further critique is of their lack of time to acquire information or think about it anyway (Dahl, 1970, pp. 42–60).

Nothing much is said in the actual studies of referendums and initiatives about the question of time. This may be for two reasons. One is that only a minority of policies gets voted on popularly, around 10 per cent or less. Time might become much more of a constraint if all important matters were put to the population. The other is that criticisms based on time constraints generally refer to face-to-face meetings held on a near-continuous basis where ordinary people are likely to drop out and leave the more extreme to take over – as Dahl (1970, p. 50) warns on the basis of experience with student meetings of the late 1960s.

Time is less of a consideration where the need for participation is sporadic and limited, as it is even in Switzerland at the present time. It may be more of a criticism to be levelled at extensions of direct democracy to cover all important decisions, in a fairly continuous manner. If debate is made more accessible through interactive television, we have, however, argued that it would have the same wide popular appeal as news programmes, current affairs and talk shows – the staple of much current television programming and sole output of successful channels like CNN.

The only direct evidence on time constraints from the studies of initiatives is of a drop-off effect from those voting for candidates to those voting on policy propositions, even on the same occasion; and a general lowering of participation (from 5 per cent to 40 per cent depending on the issue) on direct compared to representative ballots. Far from putting decisions in the hands of the more extreme, however, this leaves them to the more educated and established members of society. It is likely that any drop-off in electronically based voting would do the same, though the overall effect would probably be to increase participation generally.

The fact that the educated vote more means that those who do vote on direct legislation at the present time are better equipped to deal with decision-making. The corollary is that those who do not vote cannot cope and this may on occasions be a considerable proportion of the electorate (Linder, 1994, p. 111). Because of the complexity of wording, electors can on occasion cast their vote mistakenly – on rent control in California, for example, 82 per cent of voters apparently voted in error. Given the complex form of the ballot, voting yes meant you were against rent control and voting no meant you were for it. On this basis Magleby reaches pessimistic conclusions about the individual capacity of electors on State ballots. This is reinforced by evidence that up to a third of electors use no information source at all in voting on some initiatives (Magleby, 1984, pp. 134, 144).

To some extent, however, the evaluation of these results depends on what they are evaluated against. It is clear that voters' behaviour does not conform at all to the American Progressive reformers' image of an active interested citizenry, on the basis of which they introduced initiatives at the beginning of the century. However, it is also clear that:

1   Much voting confusion and many errors are caused by an unnecessarily complicated form of ballot. Magleby himself suggests that voting in American States would be notably more informed were voters presented with simple questions involving broad policy choices (Magleby, 1994b, p. 98) – an institutional reform simple to make and already operative elsewhere. Party guidance on how to vote would also clarify alternatives for individuals.

2   It is often not clear even to elites what relevant information on the issue would be. Even an official writing voter information pamphlets on proposition issues admitted *he* was often unclear what the 'guts' of an issue were (Cronin, 1989, p. 80). One might expect on such issues that neither officials nor State legislators display higher levels of information than electors. In many surveys, about four-fifths of electors voting on issues consider themselves 'reasonably informed' (Cronin, 1989, p. 71) – and who is qualified to query that judgement? One person's rational information-economizing is another person's ignorance, and on many issues only a very bare knowledge of certain facts is enough to permit an informed vote, particularly if the issue can be related to more general attitudinal or ideological stances. For example, a proposal to protect a specified coastline from development, or more generally to give priority to environmental considerations in policy-making, is easy to understand once cleaned of legal terminology. It can be quickly related to long-standing attitudes to economic development versus conservation or to one's own circumstances as unemployed, householder, walker etc. Decisions on tackling unemployment once it is defined as a major problem are more technical and could involve long-term consequences only visible to economists. But as economists tend to quarrel about the programmes

among themselves, public preference for an immediate resolution of perceived problems may be just as wise as controverted technical advice.

3   A further point of comparison is whether electors are any better or worse informed on ballot propositions than on candidates in representative elections. As Cronin points out (1989, p. 68), many American electors know nothing of their representative's voting record in Congress (58 per cent in one sample). Here of course party affiliation offers a good clue as to the policy positions legislators generally take. But of course so it could – and does, in Switzerland and Italy – for how to vote on policy.

Apart from the cases of admitted voting mistakes on a small minority of State ballots (due to complex drafting of the alternatives rather than individual deficiencies of electors), there seems little in the copious survey evidence for the United States and Switzerland to suggest that electors are conspicuously under-informed in relevant respects compared to other political actors. (For extensive survey evidence which supports this conclusion, see Marcus and Hanson, 1993.)

That is not to say in the context of popular consultation that they have great political knowledge, or remember relevant information once the time of decision is past (Linder, 1994, p. 111). But in terms of the bare nature of the alternatives for choice, and their immediate consequences at the time of decision, they seem to know enough (Cronin, 1989, p. 71).

Less critical analyses might term this rational information-economizing on the part of citizens, which enables them to make up their minds without excessive use of time. In the process more extensive calculations and long-term consequences may be neglected. But when even elites and technical specialists are unclear about these, why should not electors be?

Nothing is more obvious than that most electors do not measure up to the ideal of the comprehensively informed activist voter. But that is not really the point at issue. The question is whether they are equipped to decide on important policies. And on that, both the collective decisions they arrive at in the mass, and the survey information on their individual capacities – when evaluated realistically against those of other political actors – support the conclusion that they are.

This is not to say, however, that they could not be helped by

institutional and other practices designed to give them more and
better information in more easily digestible form. That is what we
consider in the next section.

5.3 Would Institutional Changes and
Electronic Technology Help?

Given the patchy nature of electors' information, their varying participation on issue ballots – much influenced by wording and complexity – and the advantages given by money in getting issues on to the
ballot and voting down those opposed to vested interests, there are
clearly grounds for improvement in current direct legislative procedures. These would be even more necessary under a full-blown direct
democracy where all important decisions were taken by popular vote.

While an extension of popular voting could carry dangers if procedural rules were not put in place, it might also provide remedies to
some current abuses simply by extending the scope and continuity of
political debate. One of the problems of current forms of direct
legislation is that they operate in the odd corners of political processes. They only impinge on electors at dramatic moments and are
not subject to much discussion or scrutiny at other times. This allows
the private 'signatures industry' to operate both in the United States
and in Switzerland, in favour of covert interests which are never fully
exposed.

The effect of having all important decisions subject to discussion
and voting as part of a reasonably continuous process would be to
expose such interests to scrutiny and possibly displace them in whole
or part by political parties. We go into this below. But clearly the
more the media carry debate and discussion the more easily accessible
information would be, both to the individuals and to groups involved. One can envisage a situation where current means of information, largely the print media and detailed information pamphlets,
were supplemented and extended by electronic means. This would
not simply be based on live screening but also on electronic print
services such as the World Wide Web (WWW), videos and other
devices more commonly associated now with entertainment.

Of course, such general coverage would not follow automatically
from the extension of direct democracy but would have to be guaranteed by procedures and rules. Here again, however, any transition to
greater participation is going to involve a rethinking of rules designed

to ensure fair coverage of issues, and giving space to all groups who have an interest in them. Such procedures are almost guaranteed by the fears and criticisms of direct democracy reviewed here, which would have to be met in any attempt to extend general participation.

If the electronic media are to be used as a forum for debate and voting, like a legislative chamber, they require a similar support apparatus to permit them to serve as a medium of discussion. No one would think of turning legislators into a hall and then expecting them to have ordered discussion and voting without a President and secretariat, no regulations limiting the participation of outside bodies, no criteria for apportioning time among participants, no rules for how long debates could continue and for voting – without even rules and committees for revising the rules in light of experience! Yet direct legislation by and large proceeds without these ancillaries. Moves to greater use of it would demand their introduction.

Particularly important would be the apportionment of time on the electronic media. This would demand not only regulation of the ownership of the channels of information, but regulation of advertising and general access to groups and parties interested in the debate, and more generally on finance and amounts of money to be spent on campaigning. Regulations would have to be supported by sanctions, possibly through the courts, but probably also through a (direct) legislative officer who would intervene as the President or Speaker of parliaments do in their proceedings – thus on a continuing and full-time basis.

Of course, given new technical developments, much discussion could be undertaken interactively and directly between interested individuals and groups. Stressing the need for regulation of central and common channels does not preclude this but complements it.

Further extensions of parliamentary safeguards to popular voting could include declarations of personal interest on the part of participants and a register of all groups and organizations involved, with a full description of their connections and motivations under penalties for false declarations. Commercial lobbying, collection of signatures and organization of campaigns would be forbidden or strictly regulated.

The possibilities for regulation and control of discussion are almost limitless and not all need be adopted. It is obvious, however, that some kind of minimal regulation of access and of opportunities for access to the major channels of communication is essential for direct democracy to work, let alone to improve the quality of popular participation. To say this is to underline the need for safeguards but hardly to criticize the system which requires them, any more than one criticizes representative democracy for having such rules in regard to parliament.

The form of ballots and of proposals to vote on is also important. Magleby (1994b, p. 98) stresses in particular the need to substitute for the complex legislative format of American State ballots a simpler and more direct form of wording, as on most referendums. The example he cites is from the British referendum on the European Community in 1975: Do you think that the United Kingdom should remain in the European Economic Community? This clearly gives an overall direction to policy, although it may leave crucial details to be decided by political actors other than the voters. As we shall see in chapter 6, much political debate *is* about the setting of priorities for which questions like this one may be perfectly adequate. The Swiss and Italians mix general questions with quite complex legislative formulations. The best way to proceed may be to make proposals as simple and direct as the matter allows; and in any case to make supporting information as clear as possible. A shift of emphasis to electronically based, visual and oral presentation, supplementing print, may help here.

Ballot proposals and referendum questions share two further characteristics:

1   They are generally confined to a single issue or issue-area. American and Swiss courts have struck down attempts to have a single vote on a package of proposals drawn from diverse areas, since they object to building a majority on a 'coalition of minorities'. As we shall see in the next chapter (when we look at structural features of voting which could affect prospects for direct democracy), the practice of confining votes to single issues could leave a majority feeling dissatisfied with the outcome as a whole, even though a majority wins on each single issue. Legislatures, however, also tend to consider policy and hold votes on single issue-areas taken separately (Shepsle and Weingast, 1981) as do governments in implementing policy (Klingemann, Hofferbert, Budge et al., 1994). Whatever distortions are introduced by individual consideration of issues are shared by both forms of democracy. In any case it can be argued that the issue-by-issue median position favoured by particular majorities *is* the best overall outcome.

2   The typical form of vote on an initiative or referendum question is yes/no. This may simplify drastically out of a range of possible options available, but does have the advantage of being easier for

voters to handle (choosing either a certain direction of change *or* the status quo). It also avoids the arbitrariness and potential instability of voting on three or more options, the so-called Condorcet cycle which we shall consider in detail in chapter 6.

Some distortions produced by the need to make choices simple for electors (not absent either from legislative practices, however) might be met by a general involvement of the political parties in direct legislation. Parties with an overall programme for government could give a lead to electors on how to vote on single issues in ways which conformed to the general programme. Single-issue voting under the guidance of parties would thus not lead to frustration with outcomes when the whole package was put together.

We shall consider the details of this in chapter 6. The important point, however, is that one should not conceive of direct democracy operating without the participation of the political parties. Commentators are indeed practically unanimous in seeing party intervention as the major way to improve the quality of individual choice on direct legislation. Parties do this in four main ways:

(1) Party endorsements provide an easy way for voters to relate a particular issue to their broad stance over a range of political issues. Though it does simplify and abstract from a much more complex underlying reality, the left–right ideological continuum offers an orientation to a range of central policy questions (opposing peace, government intervention and generally progressive policy stances on the left to a stress on order, security and minimal government on the right – Laver and Budge, 1992, pp. 25–30). Parties, even the American parties, position themselves consistently on this continuum (Klingemann, Hofferbert, Budge et al., 1994, p. 140). Thus their endorsements of or opposition to particular issues indicate to electors whether the proposal is left, centre or right, so they can relate their ballot decision to their personal ideological preference.

(2) By providing guidance of this kind parties can sketch out an overall position consistent with the general programme for government. They can thus improve the overall policy coherence of single-issue balloting by tying it in with the overall governmental programme supported at the previous election.

This is important, as one criticism of direct democracy is that single measures may often be incompatible with general policy. Parties can help to ensure their compatibility, though it must be said that the analysis of party programmes shows the internal relationship between the individual policies included there to be usually contingent, and not logically entailed. Thus the results of a whole series of measures voted in individually might be just as easy to fit together with each other and with a pre-existing programme as the priorities actually put together in a party platform itself.

We shall see this more clearly when we examine the structure of political rhetoric and of election programmes in the next chapter.

We might also observe, however, that direct legislation which contradicts a previously endorsed government programme is not necessarily bad for that reason. It shows that electors are dissatisfied with some outcomes of the programme, even if previously, and without experience of its consequences, they had voted it in. It is precisely this kind of more specific and frequent consultation that direct democracy is designed to provide in contrast to the widely separated intervals at which electors under representative democracy are allowed to make policy judgements. To criticize popular decisions for being incompatible with established government policy may miss the point. But certainly parties could help to reduce unnecessary discrepancies.

(3)   A further service parties can perform is in revealing the interests and groups involved in promoting initiatives. This is not simply a function of the more extended and informed debate that parties are likely to stimulate. Their participation means that groups and single-issue movements have to line up with parties, thus revealing their ideological preferences. Again therefore parties may provide a kind of short-hand, easily understood information to electors about the general implications of issues.

(4)   Where parties get engaged, their capacity to mobilize support and tap into a pre-existing, multi-purpose organization helps deprive well-financed interests of most of their advantages. This is shown practically in the Italian case. Interest groups were present in initiative campaigns but the parties' success in mobilizing their own supporters and in publicizing their position neutralized their advantages.

How would parties get involved in direct legislation on a comprehensive and continuing basis? As we have seen, they tend to abstain at the moment on many issues because these are marginal to their main policy goals, might create internal divisions, and do not affect their overall control of government.

However, the extension of popular voting to all important decisions would necessarily touch on central matters of party ideology, and force them to involve themselves in most ballots or lose all influence over government. This they are unlikely to do for the very reasons that cause them to compete in general elections under representative democracy.

Internal motivations based on ideological considerations and desire to keep control could of course be reinforced by regulation in a full-blown direct democracy. State funding might be made available only to groups running candidates for office who had also declared a position on all single-policy issues being voted on (or on a specified sub-set of these). More directly, groups aspiring to control government might only qualify if they had declared a position over all or most popularly voted issues.

The most obvious way one could see parties functioning in direct democracy would be to have them running candidates in general elections, as happens now, to form a government. The parties would produce a general programme whose plausibility and appeal would obviously be a factor in being elected. Policy-voting by citizens would take place between general elections but possibly under varying institutional safeguards, given that electing a government also involves considering its general programme. There could be a moratorium on raising issues certified as forming part of the government programme, for a certain period of time after the general election. Or government positions could be protected by requiring absolute or qualified majorities for their rejection, as suggested in chapter 2.

Whatever institutional safeguards (or none) for the general programme were adopted, the government would clearly be bound to give a lead to electors in supporting or opposing measures which centrally affected it. Doing so would draw in its constituent parties and probably the opposition. Given the loose-knit nature of most party programmes, the government could live with defeats on some of its measures. With too many it might have to threaten an election and seek a popular vote of confidence, as it does now with legislatures.

On the other side of the equation, electors are clearly predisposed to follow party and governmental guidance, as the strong discrepancies between the success rates of initiatives with and without government sponsorship shows in both the US and Switzerland (Magleby, 1994b, p. 93; Kriesi, 1994, p. 70; Linder, 1994, pp. 99–100). This guards against any possible cyclical effects, where a new dissatisfied popular majority votes down proposals previously passed by an earlier majority. There is no evidence of this actually happening anywhere, but party loyalties would be an additional safeguard against it.

Thus there is no doubt about the institutional practicability of having party government, and party leads on single issues, under direct democracy. Nor, given the analyses of existing direct legislation, is there much doubt of the desirability of parties playing a role, and providing the benefits listed immediately above. The main question, again in light of the actual findings in Switzerland and the United States, is whether parties might not be so seriously weakened by having to cope with direct legislation that they simply could not perform an organizing and guiding role nor survive as political actors. This is the alarming possibility we now consider.

5.4 Are Parties Weakened by Participation?

After the various discussions in this book there is no need to re-emphasize that modern democracy, whether representative or direct, is above all party democracy. Parties give a lead on how to vote on candidates and policy, stimulate debate, encourage participation and manage government. Without them there would be confusion at electoral level and chaos at governmental level, and no obvious way of linking the two. The criticism that greater participation weakens parties is therefore a very serious one. What is the evidence for it?

There is no doubt that a majority of commentators on direct legislation in the American States and in Switzerland do consider that it weakens political parties. They see it as doing so in four ways:

1 By removing some legislative matters from the control of the governing party. In particular, decisions are forced on matters neither raised nor framed by the parties.
2 As a consequence of this, it reduces the coherence and consistency of the policy package that the ruling party is trying to promote.
3 Single-issue groups are more extreme and less compromising than political parties, so popular consultations encourage the taking of extreme positions and reduce the possibility of negotiation and agreement.
4 Leaders may take opposing sides in popular consultations and electors may ignore or even defy the party lead where it is given.

This is particularly emphasized by Kobach (1994, p. 132) for Switzerland.

These conclusions are by no means incontrovertible, however, and to some extent are inconsistent among themselves. The description of internal dissension at leadership and electoral level, produced by popular consultation, is simply contradicted by other commentators (e.g. Kriesi, 1994, pp. 71–3) who see electors following a clear party lead when it is consistent with its ideology. Factionalism among the leaders can be regarded as a normal facet of parties which appears frequently in parliaments as well as in initiatives and referendums. Indeed, by deliberately keeping out of some areas not central to their ideology, parties may be able to *preserve* overall unity and thus *strengthen* themselves in many cases, as Butler and Ranney point out (1994, p. 260). Coherence and consistency are in the eye of the beholder and not particularly evident inside government programmes themselves, even where not affected by direct legislation.

On possibilities of negotiation and compromise, the commentators again contradict each other. In the American case Magleby (1984, pp. 188–90) emphasizes the confrontational aspects of direct legislation, and Cronin (1989, p. 248) sees compromise and negotiations as a distinct advantage of parliamentary processes. Yet if the policy-outcomes of direct legislation do not differ much from those produced by legislators, does the contrast in tactics and style really matter? The Swiss commentators unanimously see referendums and initiatives as a major element in promoting consultation and reducing conflict. In Italy, parliamentary compromises went so far as to block most decisions, and popular consultations provided a rare opportunity to take authoritative steps which were then generally accepted.

Much of the problem in judging the effects of direct democracy on parties stems from the lack of a clear criterion by which to evaluate party behaviour. Is it to be compared with some abstract model of a political party, with a disciplined body of electors following a unified leadership based on a coherent underlying ideology and published policy? The American literature emphasizes the first two aspects. Because the modern parties in States with direct legislation are not the highly organized and centralized political machines of the beginning of the century, parties are taken as having been weakened.

Yet one might claim they have simply adapted to new conditions. There is no sign in any American State of traditional parties losing control of elective offices. And they continue to influence the central policies of government as much as they ever have done.

Perhaps in fact, as was done with policy-outcomes, one should compare parties in States with direct legislation and those without, to see if there is a real difference in party standing and authority. If such a comparison is made, it is very difficult to detect any systematic pattern of differences. Indeed, the major change in the position of State-level parties has been the breakdown of one-party dominance in the South, regardless of whether direct legislation existed or not. And this has strengthened parties rather than weakened them.

Direct legislation and party competition has helped in the creation of more meaningful competition by offering opportunities for the minority party, usually the Republicans, to make its name known at State level by sponsoring initiatives (Magleby, 1994b, pp. 88, 94). This is a phenomenon also noted in Switzerland and Italy and runs counter to some of the pessimistic conclusions noted above. Minority and opposition parties are able to use initiatives to establish themselves. This is surely a contribution to the revitalization of parties rather than to their decline.

Perhaps, however, initiatives weaken established and government parties? Indeed the comments highlighted at the beginning of this section do seem preoccupied with established parties, even if they then over-generalize their concerns to parties as such. It is important to break this false equivalence in reaching balanced conclusions about the effects of popular consultations on parties.

If one does look at established parties, however, one can repeat the question of how far they are really weakened by popular consultations in comparison to the particular set of representative institutions within which they operate. The separation of powers in American States, often producing a divided Executive and Legislature and the need to work with cross-party coalitions, is surely a greater influence on the structure of State parties than any provision for direct legislation. Working with political opponents causes parties to opt out of some issues and refuse to take responsibility for others, while legislative compromises reduce the coherence of their programme – precisely the effects attributed to direct legislation but no more evident in States with it than without it.

Similar effects flow from the need to form a governmental coalition in Switzerland. Swiss politics are, however, less messy than those of

Belgium – a country with coalitions but without popular consultation. Parties have split linguistically in Belgium but not in Switzerland. Similarly in Italy, it was governmental paralysis and corruption on a massive scale that broke the Christian Democrats and Socialists, not the impact of initiatives, whose contribution was rather to ameliorate the negative aspects of politics under the old regime. This in turn allowed the old parties to stagger on until in effect they destroyed themselves.

On the positive side, popular initiatives draw parties' attention to new issues, enabling them to maintain or extend their appeal by incorporating these in their programmes. They provide a dynamic for the growth of new parties, which is also an important element in the development and revitalization of existing parties. Many single-issue movements, by participating in a range of policy ballots, develop a comprehensive programme and thus transform themselves into parties which run candidates – the Greens, for example. When established parties refuse to share power or concede demands, the initiative allows excluded groups to force their way into negotiations and sometimes too into government.

These are not negligible effects of direct legislation, and the point is that they aid the emergence and consolidation of political parties rather than weakening them. There is a considerable inconsistency among commentators, all of whom concur on the help given by popular campaigning to minority opposition parties. Most, however, do not see this as a contribution to party strength in general because they identify this with the dominance of established parties. That is misleading. Even in the case of older parties, however, the effects of popular discussion and competition, while refreshing, have hardly affected their governmental position. They may have lost some voters to new rivals, but that loss has occurred in all the representative democracies of the world, so it can hardly be attributed to direct popular involvement in a few of them.

This, however, raises another possibility in regard to modern parties. Let us grant that direct legislation as such may have few or marginal effects. Is it not the case, however, that certain trends – above all the development of the electronic media which renders interactive popular consultations possible – have fatally weakened the strength of political parties everywhere? If that is so, we need not wait for the actual onset of direct democracy to see parties crumble, as this may be happening already. Given the stress we have placed on the need for political parties to guide participation, allegations of their general decline would indeed strike at the heart of the arguments supporting its extension. Accordingly, we examine the evidence for general party decline in the next section.

5.5 Party Decline or Business as Usual?

Being so central to modern political life, individual parties are often subject to dramatic ups and downs. Though the effects are temporary, the circumstances usually strike commentators so forcibly that they generalize one or two individual events into a secular tendency affecting all parties (generally in a negative way).

Thus the famous Bad Godesberg programme, with which in 1959 the German Social Democrats renounced their adherence to Marxist principles, was immediately interpreted as the 'End of Ideology' (Bell, 1960) for all political parties and as heralding the advent of a new kind of non-ideological 'catch-all' party which abandoned its traditional support groups and sought votes from everywhere (Kircheimer, 1966).

Events overtook these theses as ideological divisions hardened in the 1970s and 1980s and separated even the American Republicans and Democrats (Klingemann, Hofferbert, Budge et al., 1994, pp. 136–54). By 1983 the German Social Democrats were as far to the left in terms of policy as they had been in 1953 (Budge, 1994, pp. 458–9).

These let-downs warn us against over-dramatizing and over-generalizing from particular events and teach caution about seeing a 'decline of parties' emerging from the renewed activity of single-issue movements in the 1980s or from the television-based candidacies of Perot and Berlusconi in the 1990s. Even the spectacular election collapse of a government party like the Progressive Conservatives in Canada in 1993, when they declined from nearly 200 seats to three, could well be reversed in the future, as it owes much to the way the election system, under certain distributions of vote, distorts the relationship with parliamentary seats.

As opposed to spectacular but isolated events, we face the reality that, in all democracies, governments are controlled by political parties (even, as we saw, in Switzerland). Moreover, as new democracies have emerged in Mediterranean and latterly Eastern Europe, their politics have been organized primarily around party competition – in keeping with the general argument of this book that it is impossible to organize modern democracies without it.

With relatively weak social structures and a highly personalized executive Presidency, both the ex-Soviet and Latin American countries have produced less institutionalized and weaker party structures than elsewhere. But it is notable that even in such a situation candidates feel the need to create a personal organization modelled on the party which may indeed outlast its founder and become an institution with policy-making and electoral capabilities of its own.

This situation is not dissimilar to what commentators have seen happening with American parties, where the power of central bosses based on an efficient party organization and on the distribution of office and patronage has been broken. It has been succeeded by a much more open (and, it must be said, democratic) situation inside both parties. Now individual candidates build up a personal campaign organization, make alliances with supporting interest groups, and fight for the party nomination in internal party elections ('primaries') where all those declaring an affiliation with the party can vote. This has been seen as evidence of the decline of the party into a kind of shell organization, simply a framework for the operation of more significant groups (Pomper, 1980).

From an Italian or Japanese perspective, however, where most parties have at least two permanent internal factions with recognized leaders and organization, these tendencies seem neither unfamiliar nor threatening. The overall organization, dominance of which is the goal of internal factional struggle, continues to impose unity and get support from most of its members most of the time. The party label matters to candidates and they run on the same policy platform. Factions are simply one mode of party organization which may serve to maximize finance or ·votes. It is not the end of parties since (a) many parties coexist with them quite happily over long periods of time; (b) where it becomes extreme, factions may split off and become parties on their own account. This is not the end of parties but simply another change in the party system.

Meanwhile many single-issue organizations extend their appeal and organize as political parties, developing an across-the-board programme and running candidates, as the Greens did in the 1980s.

In all these developments one can trace changes in party organization and forms of electioneering, as well as greater volatility on the part of electors between individual parties. But nothing necessarily betokens a decline of parties as such. Rather, change and adaptation, as well as a replacement of some parties by others, can be taken as evidence of the vitality of party systems and the continuing dominance of parties as institutions.

We need to explore these points further, starting with an attempt to specify what the 'decline of the political party' might entail, and seeing whether these consequences are actually apparent in contemporary democracies. The trouble with talking about decline is that parties are very much multi-level and multi-faceted organizations, centred around ideology and policy, but also characterized by candidates, personalities and organizations. As institutions, they can embrace at least seven sets of phenomena:

1 The top party leadership, whose concern is with strategy and immediate political problems, as they may form the government. Leaders may be reasonably united or permanently factionalized – both situations are normal and can continue for long periods. Even at the best of times there will be strong personal rivalries among individuals, exacerbated by competition for the top position.
2 A parliamentary group linked to leaders, and itself possibly united or prone to split into factions.
3 A bureaucratic organization devoted to research, finances, campaign management etc.
4 Party activists and workers, usually formally enrolled in the party and organized on a territorial basis.
5 Specialist groups, women, workers, farmers, youth – who may have quite strong semi-autonomous organizations within the party.
6 Party voters, themselves falling into the two groups of regular supporters and adherents, and those who vote more casually and occasionally for the party.
7 Ideology set down in books, pamphlets, constitutions and other documents, which is to a greater or lesser extent shared by all the foregoing groupings.

In keeping with the general tendency among commentators to (over)react to dramatic events, change at one of these levels is often identified with decline, while developments at the others are ignored. Thus the perceived abandonment of ideology in the 1960s was often linked to a perceived decline of the party *per se*. (As parties became mere managers of government, interest groups would dominate in neo-corporatist policy-making (Schmitter and Lehmbruch, 1979).)

The re-emergence of ideological divisions in the 1980s has often been interpreted as a victory of the Right, while Socialist parties are now seen as having abandoned their true inheritance at some variously dated point in the past and as losing their true justification. (For comparative analyses of programmes showing that on the contrary they have stayed just where they always were, see Budge and Farlie, 1977, pp. 424–5; Laver and Budge, 1992, *passim*; Klingemann, Hofferbert, Budge et al., 1994, *passim*.)

Similarly, voting changes and in particular greater volatility between parties are interpreted as evidence of declining electoral loyalty to parties (Franklin, Mackie and Valen, 1992), ignoring the fact that when voters switch they vote for *other* parties. Again, we see here this general tendency to identify the fate of parties with that of *established* parties, which is not necessarily the same thing. As von Beyme (1985, p. 305) remarks, much depends on the capacity of new parties to absorb the voters who move and on the capacity of the system to accommodate new parties. So far they have shown a marked ability to do this.

It is certainly true that popular expressions of strong attachment to parties have gone down, and the numbers of electors describing themselves as 'strong identifiers' with political parties has declined in both Britain and the United States. In a discipline dominated by English-speaking analysts and commentators, this finding has had a disproportionate influence over debate (cf. Wattenburg, 1990). Yet it remains true that in other countries (Spain, Portugal, Greece and France) the number of identifiers has gone up. Moreover, American electors, however they may characterize themselves, keep on voting Democrat and Republican. The incursions of non-party candidates are limited at all levels, and the traditional parties monopolize State and Federal offices. The Republicans, with the redefinition of their ideology, have had a renaissance everywhere but particularly in the South, where they had not been competitive for 100 years.

These considerations underline the point made above, that parties are complex multi-level organizations. This indeed is what makes them so unique and valuable, as they are the only institutions that tie governments into large popular groupings. Thus it is particularly dangerous to concentrate on only one aspect or level of their activities. Trends can well go in opposite directions and constitute regrouping and necessary adaptation rather than irreversible decline.

This is especially evident in discussions of party membership. Particularly since the advent of the mass party in Europe (Duverger,

1951) large numbers of members have been regarded as a sign of viability for a party. The marked fall in their numbers over the post-war period in Britain has thus been taken as a conclusive indication of decline. However, this cannot be generalized (von Beyme, 1985, p. 188). In some countries, membership has increased. Moreover, in many countries, including Britain, the parties have expanded their activities in local government and created a new figure, the activist devoted to local politics, in many ways more experienced and valuable to the party than the old doorstep campaigner.

However, the broader point is that parties existed, under other conditions, as parties of notables who organized their own campaigns before changed circumstances required mass support. Under other conditions therefore parties could survive a drastically reduced membership. Indeed, such an adaptation has already been happening as parties discovered they could campaign directly through the media and put recruitment much lower on their list of priorities. The reduction in membership, where it has occurred, is in part due to a different leadership strategy.

This again reminds us that in considering parties we cannot simply concentrate on any one level or any one indicator of vitality or health. In a judicious review of 'The Changing West European Mass Party', Peter Mair (1992) sees much more evidence of change and adaptation than of decline. Indeed, as he remarks, we hardly have the data about all the aspects of parties which are relevant, to spot decline if it were actually occurring. The most obvious phenomenon is the continued dominance of parties over governments and over electoral competition, where the activities of non-party candidates hardly make a dent, in any democracy in the world (von Beyme, 1985, p. 372). Established parties may occasionally go down, but old rivals or new succeed them, often injecting party competition with new vigour. The best prognosis is that this will continue, even if the mass membership party is succeeded (but only in part) by organizations much more centred on the uses that can be made of the media, of which the now looser-knit but more ideologically focused American parties may be the forerunners.

5.6 Parties under (and with) Direct Democracy

In the current situation, then, parties seem to be flourishing, and they are more likely to be weakened by institutional practices at legislative level than by direct legislation. Our argument, however, goes beyond the actual functioning of contemporary parties to how they would operate under a full-blown direct democracy. So we have to consider here what parties would look like if popular participation were drastically extended – to voting on all the important decisions now taken by legislatures.

We have emphasized the need for such voting to be organized and guided by political parties. But could parties themselves remain un-changed under such a transition? The evidence already reviewed suggests they would *survive*. But would they be internally modified? In what way? And would this affect the efficiency with which they could put forward policy alternatives and play a role in government?

Were formal popular participation to be extended at the level of the nation-state, beyond voting in general elections to taking decisions on specific policy questions, it would not formally or necessarily affect non-State bodies like parties. Where these are hierarchically organized vehicles for a leadership team to attain national office, they could legally remain so. Clearly, however, the extension of democracy at national level would create demands for its extension to other political organizations. This would involve interest groups and per-haps even businesses, but also political parties, which stand in a more direct and visible relationship with the State. Thus a greater democra-tization of the State as a whole would inevitably create pressure for an internal democratization of parties. There would be a psychological and social link between the two regardless of the fact that party democratization is not logically entailed by State-wide participation.

This could have serious implications if we accept Schumpeter's paradox (1950) that parties *need* to be internally authoritarian and hierarchical if they are to present clear cut alternatives between which the democratic public can authoritatively choose. This argument follows from Schumpeter's conception of democratic choice as being between two leadership teams with different policies and personnel, competing to form a government. In this situation it is important that the party position should not be fudged, as it would be if the party had internally competing leaderships offering different policy-descriptions and each claiming to speak on its behalf. Then indeed the public would be deprived of a clear choice, having to associate each party with a range of positions and having to choose between the sets of policies offered by each side.

This contrast is developed by Wright (1971, pp. 17–54), who offers a typology of the 'rational-efficient' party as described by Schumpeter on the one hand, oriented to competing and winning elections in a competitive two-party framework, and the European, ideological and internally democratic party on the other hand, whose object is quite different – to anticipate and model the kind of political society prescribed by its ideology, without much regard to current election success.

These ideal types have in fact influenced the assessments of contemporary parties under direct legislation made above. Many of the negative judgements made about the effects of mass participation on internal party divisions are based on the idea that parties *ought* to be united around a single leadership team. In actual fact, as I have pointed out, parties in practice are rarely hierarchical and monolithic. Yet democratic choice and party competition seem to proceed perfectly well even when they are not. This observation must lead to some doubts as to whether Schumpeter and his successors (notably Downs, 1957) have been wholly correct in characterizing the prerequisites for making clear-cut electoral choices in elections.

Reinforcing this is the fact that the parties in what are widely regarded as model democracies – the countries of Scandinavia and North-West Europe – practise a very advanced type of internal party democracy. This is particularly true of Social Democratic and Labour parties. In the Netherlands, for example, statements of party policy go down to the lowest levels for debate and approval and are debated by all levels up to the Party Conference, where amended resolutions are put to a final vote. In Ireland the branches and general conference of the Labour Party have a veto over whether the party should enter a governmental coalition. The examples are far from the Schumpeterian ideal of the leadership determining the party position, and they do cause internal divisions and conflict. Yet the democracies concerned seem to function very well with it.

Part of the answer is that these countries, like most democracies but unlike the Westminster-style democracy envisaged by Schumpeter, have multi-party systems where no one party can attract a majority. Thus electoral choices are always likely to be mediated by coalition negotiations, so the importance of having clear stands by parties at elections is diminished anyway.

A more important reason, however, is that the policies offered by all parties, whether in a multi-party or two-party majority system, are shaped and bounded by their ideology. Ideology – Socialism, neo-Liberalism, Christian Democracy – is what attracts leaders and activists to the party in the first place and continues to keep them there.

These common views of the world keep intra-party disputes relatively limited therefore, confining them to immediate strategic matters and minor divergencies over emphases and wording. While these may seem very important to the persons involved, they seem relatively unimportant from the standpoint of the other parties and ideologies. Studies of party policy movements in twenty countries over the post-war period show that political parties almost always maintain the same ideological positions in relation to each other and in fact change policy remarkably little (Budge, 1994).

There is thus no need for unquestioned leadership dominance inside political parties, since their ideology defines them very well and offers electors extremely clear choices, however much internal debate and factionalism there may be. If really serious disputes occur, the party splits, and the two new parties offer electors a new choice.

Internal party democracy is thus perfectly compatible with the functioning of the overall democracy at national level. It is the permanent ideology (a factor ignored both by Schumpeter, 1950, and Downs, 1957) which guarantees clear choice; and as all adherents of the party are committed to this it is unlikely to be substantially changed by disputes among them. The ideology extends beyond general positioning at governmental elections to stands on a range of specific issues and so would be operative in direct as well as representative democracies.

If participation in national decision-making is a good thing, so also must be participation in party decisions. The basing of democratic self-justifications on the freedom offered to as many persons as possible to express their opinions and vote extends to all levels of society and its institutions (for further discussion of the various democratic arenas see section 6.4). Thus internal democracy within parties, as within businesses, bureaucracies and pressure groups, must be a good thing in the absence of countervailing considerations. The major such consideration in the case of parties is whether it might not prevent them offering clear-cut policy choices at the level of the political unit they are operating in – offering a way for electors to economize on the information-processing and calculations they would have to make to come to a rational decision. As such choices are, however, determined by party ideology and the associated government record rather than the immediate decisions they make, there is absolutely no objection to them being as internally democratic as they please. It would, from a participatory point of view, be a good thing if they were. Ultimately the contrast between rational-efficient and ideologically based, internally democratic parties is a false one since being ideological and democratic strengthens the overall democracy in which they function.

5.7 Conclusions

In this chapter we have spent time reviewing the conclusions that can be drawn from contemporary experience with popular voting on policies. Given that no disasters have occurred and that the effects indeed have been moderately beneficial, readers may well feel that too much time has been spent on the review. Commentators are, however, so inclined to make sweeping generalizations about popular ignorance or party decline that we must see in detail how far these assertions are supported by their evidence.

In fact we find they have little support. Voters seem reasonably competent to make judgements on policy and certainly as competent as they are to make judgements on candidates. What voter confusion and error there is derives from institutional practices (like not putting party guidance on ballot papers) which could easily be changed. This applies also to more active party participation in policy-voting campaigns.

With regard to parties themselves, the most obvious conclusion is that they are in rude health, active everywhere, endlessly adapting to new political circumstances, and hence monopolizing government office and electoral competition. Fears for their survival simply fly in the face of the facts or base themselves on unsubstantiated speculation about the long-term effects of the media (cf. Zolo, 1992, pp. 162–70). So far parties have shown themselves perfectly capable of adapting first to newspapers, then to radio and television. The latter may require changes which we see working their way through today, such as moves to more internal democracy. But these are evidence of adaptation rather than decline, and perfectly compatible with parties' role in organizing and focusing policy-decisions.

There is therefore no reason to doubt the ability of parties to guide popular voting and discussion (as they already do in Switzerland and Italy and to some extent in American States), not even when it takes the form of more complex, two-way, electronic interactions on individual issues. Their participation can improve popular debate and decision-making so that it contributes constructively to the government of society – which will, for the foreseeable future, remain in the hands of political parties.

6

Structural Problems and Constraints

6.1 Introduction

While parties may improve the quality of information available to policy-voters, and guide their choices, can they overcome the structural problems which may be inherent in direct voting and may render its outcomes arbitrary or inconclusive? Structural problems were discussed briefly in chapter 3 but require more extended consideration here. This is because they have become increasingly central to the whole theory of democratic decision-making since their rediscovery in the post-war period (Arrow, 1951, following work by Borda, 1784, and Condorcet, 1785; see also Black, 1958).

Their importance derives from the alarming possibility that democratic voting procedures may either prove incapable of producing any clear majority at all, or only produce one by arbitrary means which favour some entrenched minority at the expense of others. How this happens we shall consider in the next section.

If such problems afflicted all forms of democratic voting equally, we would not have to bother about them, as they would not enter into choices between representative and direct democracy. It has been argued, however, that they affect popular voting for policies rather than popular voting for candidates (Riker, 1982) and thus provide strong arguments in favour of representative arrangements. Or, more subtly, it has been suggested that, as they would affect popular policy voting, as much as any other kind of voting, there is no point in getting too enthusiastic about it even if the problems occur with other forms as well (McLean, 1989).

These arguments are of a different kind to the ones about the practical operation of direct democracy which we have been considering. They tend to undermine the central justification put forward in chapter 1 for extending popular involvement in decision-making, which was based on the need for ever greater consent to what democratic government does in many situations. For if in many situations one cannot get genuine consent to any decision, or if consent has to be manipulated to get a decision, it becomes much less appealing as a quality to be maximized by popular participation. Perhaps, as McLean hints, it is just not worth the trouble of looking for it (McLean, 1989, pp. 112–29; Riker, 1982, p. 238).

Why this might be we shall consider below, presenting the structural problems of aggregating votes in their general form, and showing how they follow from perfectly democratic assumptions about the voting procedures to be followed. In section 6.3, however, we shall look more closely at these assumptions and ask whether they are entirely correct about the way people discuss policy and vote on it. Given that parties are so central to the governance and functioning of direct democracy, it is appropriate to look at the way they structure political discussion.

It does seem in fact that, in order to economize on time and information, parties discuss each individual policy on its own in ways which avoid at least some problems of aggregating votes. Since they are as or more likely to do this under direct as under representative democracy, the former is unlikely to produce inconclusive or arbitrary decisions to any greater extent than representative forms.

This analysis of policy-related discourse and decision-making forms the background to our consideration of another long-standing problem about democratic consent, the question of minorities faced with a decision they have not voted for. Can they be said to have consented to it in any way? If not, how can they be said to be bound by it? While it may not resolve this problem, the idea of political discussion as involving priorities rather than sharply opposed preferences helps to suggest that many in the minority may endorse goals they have voted against prioritizing at the present time and thus in a broad way may not oppose even when they have voted against them. Too often this question has been discussed at a highly abstract level, so suggestions that the minority might consent in some way to decisions they have voted against have remained vague and faintly menacing. (Their consent can be inferred from their opposition!) By tying it to the specific patterns of democratic political discourse, we hope here to make it more concrete and less sinister.

These considerations apply to minorities which find themselves outvoted on a particular issue or perhaps in a specific policy-area. They have less relevance where a minority is permanent and distinguished by some prominent socioeconomic difference from the majority (linguistic, racial, religious, territorial or even class-related). In situations where they are regularly outvoted over a series of issues which affect them crucially, it is less obvious that they consent in any way to what the majority are imposing on them.

In this situation the only solution may well be the secession of the minority to form their own direct democracy, separate from the original one at any rate on the crucial issues affecting the minority. This point brings us on to the question of the entities within which direct democracy might operate – territorial like existing States; functional like a firm or other territorially dispersed pre-existing groupings; or personally chosen and voluntaristic associations.

A further question linked to the problem of defining boundaries for direct democracies is how far their powers may be limited or decisions usurped by their place in a world hierarchy of organizations, whether these be nation-states, military alliances, multinational corporations or markets. Are the constraints imposed by the international order so great as to vitiate decisions taken lower down, thus rendering popular participation at lower levels a sham and illusion? What might be done about it? And what consequences might this have for direct democracy at the national and local level where it is usually discussed? Can one conceive of transnational, regional or even world arrangements based on direct democracy as described here? (For a rare discussion of the international situation from a concern with democracy see Held, 1993b, pp. 13–52.)

Clearly such wide extensions of popular participation would not be immediate developments, so a primary focus in this discussion is how national and local democracies would be constrained by current international developments. These could affect direct democracy as severely as the internal structural constraints on the aggregation of preferences, with which we begin the next section.

6.2 Possible Paradoxes of Democratic Voting Procedures

These paradoxes, already briefly mentioned in chapter 3, derive ultimately from two basic assumptions:

1 There will usually be more than two alternatives to vote on (whether these are candidates in an election or policy options on an issue is irrelevant at a formal level of discussion).
2 Electors will vote on the basis of a rank-ordering of the alternatives on offer: most preferred ranked first (1), next most preferred second (2), next most preferred (3).

Preferences between alternatives might be indicated by a simple ordering (ABC when alternative A is preferred to B and both over C). Or numerals might be assigned to them (shown within parentheses above) indicating most preferred, second most preferred etc.

We should note that there are really two assumptions here which are usually conflated with each other in the notion of electors voting on a preference-schedule, as this rank-ordering is called. The first is that individuals operate on the basis of this ordering in deciding for themselves how to vote – that is, that they do not score the alternatives more exactly in some way in deciding how to vote on them but simply rank them mentally.

The second is that alternatives cannot in any case be assigned a public score by electors, however they may have arrived at their individual decision. Public preferences can only be expressed by rankings because scoring systems would differ between individuals. Using the only 'public' scoring system, and denominating preferences in terms of money, would be inappropriate. If everyone voted by paying a certain sum to have alternatives chosen, the rich who could afford more would have much more say in the decision, thus violating democratic rules of equality.

For these reasons the discussion proceeds in terms of voters' individual rankings of alternatives. There are three major ways of aggregating these:

(1) By taking only first preferences and choosing the one that gets most votes. This has the disadvantages that the winning alternative is not guaranteed majority support and may indeed be strongly opposed by a majority. It also ignores preferences between the other alternatives and may lead to a tie where first preferences aggregate to equal amounts for each alternative. Ties could be broken by chance (throwing dice) or arbitrarily. A more appealing alternative might be to take the whole rank-ordering into account, in which case the other procedures listed below come into play.

(2)   The first of these to be suggested historically (Borda, 1784) was to use the rank-orders to aggregate scores. Scoring the last preference of each voter as number 'a' (usually 0), second last $a + b$ (b is usually 1), third last $a + 2b$ etc. gives scores to each alternative which reflect voters' individual ordering. These 'Borda counts' can then be added over all voters and the alternative with the highest score selected.

Note that by adding rank-orders in this way the procedure makes assumptions which in effect transform them into cardinal numbers. The difference between candidates ranked 1 and 2 is assumed to be the same for all voters, although for one voter it could be much larger than for another. And even for the same voter the distance between rank-orders 1 and 2 could be much greater than between the candidates ranked 3 and 4. We do not know, and the assumption of equal intervals is the easiest to make. But it is quite as arbitrary as any other assumption about distances that we care to make, and does transform the ordinal information into something resembling a numeric scoring system. We shall return to this point in section 6.4.

Borda counts do in a broad sense reflect the preferences of as many people as possible (Dummett, 1984, p. 142). However, apart from their assumptions about scoring, they have two problems:

(i)   They can be manipulated. For example, by 'strategic' voters placing the strongest rival to their most preferred choice at the bottom of their orderings. Or a stalking horse can be run who then drops out, as shown in table 6.1. The scores in table 6.1(a) with D as one of the alternatives make C the winner but in table 6.1(b) – D has been withdrawn and did not stand a chance anyway – A wins. Clearly the power of an irrelevant and hopeless alternative to affect the choice of winner is not what we want from a voting system. Of course, such a result might occur accidentally or for perfectly fair reasons rather than as a result of manipulation. This possibility however points to a desirable quality of a voting procedure being that it should not be manipulable or be affected by strategic voting, that is, it should not be affected by the inclusion and withdrawal of irrelevant alternatives (like D in table 6.1).

(ii)   Borda counts may not always select the alternative which would have won in a series of votes with other alternatives. This is illustrated in table 6.2 which was produced by Condorcet (1785, pp. cxxvii–clxxix) as a criticism of the voting procedure advocated by Borda. A 'Condorcet winner' is an alternative which can beat every other alternative when each is compared in turn with all the others.

Table 6.1 The effect of irrelevant alternatives on the Borda count

(a)				
No. voters	30	20	20	
	A	B	C	
	B	C	D	
	C	D	A	
	D	A	B	
Borda count	A110	B120	C130	D60
(b)				
No. voters	30	20	20	
	A	B	C	
	B	C	A	
	C	A	B	
Borda count	A80	B70	C60	

A, B, C and D are policy-alternatives being voted on by electorate. As can be seen from the table, D is an alternative/candidate which does not attract much support and has no hope of winning.

Table 6.2 An example of the failure of a Borda count to select a majority winner

No. voters	30	1	10	29	10	1
	A	A	C	B	B	C
	B	C	A	A	C	B
	C	B	B	C	A	A

Borda count: A, 101; B, 109; C, 33. Therefore B wins by Borda's rule. But the results of pairwise votes would be A v. B, 41/40 to A; A v. C, 60/21 to A; B v. C, 69/12 to B. Therefore A is the majority (Condorcet) winner.

Source: McLean (1989, p. 54), based on Condorcet (1785, pp. clxxvii–clxxix); notation mostly from Black (1958, pp. 176–7).

(3) This suggests another voting procedure in which each alternative is compared in turn with each of the others, and the one which secures a majority of preferences over all these confrontations, a 'Condorcet winner', is then chosen. As McLean (1989, p. 55) observes:

democracy involves each vote being weighted equally . . . this puts the concept of a Condorcet winner at [its] heart. A Condorcet winner is unquestionably the majority choice. To reject a Condorcet winner is to choose somebody who would lose a majority vote to the Condorcet winner. It is therefore to favour the minority against the majority.

There is an argument that strict majoritarian decision-making is not necessarily preferable under all circumstances compared to getting as close to the wishes of as many people as possible (Miller, 1993, p. 87). Table 6.2 actually illustrates this: as A wins over B by only one vote in a pairwise confrontation, the choice between them is obviously very close and B appeals more to more electors compared to A.

However, reflecting the wishes of the majority is obviously important in a democracy. Unfortunately, these may not always be reflected by Condorcet procedures. This follows from the following considerations:

(i)   Condorcet procedures are also open to manipulation. An example is given by Miller (1993, p. 80), in a choice of energy options, in which nuclear power is the Condorcet winner if everyone votes sincerely. Someone strongly committed to coal might stop the nuclear option by voting insincerely for gas when the choice between nuclear power and gas comes up, thus preventing the emergence of a nuclear winner and hoping, in the resulting unstructured situation, that coal may win.

(ii)   A further difficulty with Condorcet procedures is that no clear majority winner may emerge. In table 6.1(b) it is clear that, in a series of pairwise comparisons, A wins over B (50–20): B wins over C (50–20) but C wins over A (40–30). There is thus no clear winner: everything depends on the order of voting and the specific procedures employed (e.g. if the C-B vote was held first and then the B-A vote, nobody would be in much doubt that A had won, but if the sequence were the other way round, B would win).

The possibility of such voting cycles has been a central topic in discussions of democratic voting procedures ever since their rediscovery in the 1950s. The central justification for democracy of whatever form is the fact that it allows popular preferences to be expressed, whether on governments, policies or both. If their expression often results in incoherent or unstable outcomes, how can democracy truly claim to express popular feeling? And if it does not, should one not turn to other, less arbitrary and more binding ways of getting collective discussions through authoritative procedures of some kind which at least guarantee a result? The dilemma is particularly acute since the binary Condorcet votes which produce cycles are the procedures best adapted to get a genuine majority choice which, as McLean says, is at the heart of democratic practices.

Obviously, in evaluating voting procedures, we want to know how often manipulation and voting cycles are likely to occur. Mathematical work on these points, based on the assumptions we have stated, reaches alarming conclusions.

First, Gibbard (1973) and Satterthwaite (1975) demonstrate that every voting system is liable to be manipulated, that is, it is unable always to guarantee that increasing popularity of an option among individual voters does not actually diminish its chance of success, since it cannot guard adequately against strategic addition or withdrawal of options to be voted on.

This proof was actually a corollary of work by Kenneth Arrow (1951) which shows that no voting procedure can guarantee a winning alternative which could not be beaten by some other alternative, if it meets some very minimal and eminently democratic conditions of fairness. These conditions are that:

1   The procedure must cope with every possible individual ordering of preferences. This is very democratic as everyone's preferences ought to have an equal weight determining outcomes. As we have seen, some combinations of individual orderings will not produce an unbeatable winner, however, so the procedure will always break down and produce cycles at some point. This is not to say of course that in many circumstances it will not actually produce a Condorcet winner, only that it cannot guarantee this.

2   If every individual prefers a given alternative (w) to another (z), the social ordering should prefer w to z. But in fact a series of binary votes might not produce this outcome, as illustrated in table 6.3.

3   The overall ranking of any two alternatives should depend only on individual rankings of the two and is unaffected by 'irrelevant' third alternatives being either inserted or withdrawn. The way in which the Borda count is affected by this has already been illustrated in table 6.1.

4   There is no person whose preferences prevail regardless of anyone else's. If there were, that would solve the problem of getting determinate social choices, but at the cost of dictatorship. A possible way of avoiding dictatorship might be to adopt 'stochastic' democracy, where one person, different on each vote, is selected by lot to make the choice. Selection by lot was used quite often in the ancient world instead of election to choose people for office though not for policy-

Table 6.3 An alternative may not win even if everyone prefers it to the winner

No. voters	1	1	1
	y	x	w
	x	w	z
	w	z	y
	z	y	x

First x is paired with w and wins. Then y is paired with x and wins. Then z is paired with y and wins. But w would have been unanimously preferred to z.

Source: McLean (1989, p. 166) as adapted from Plott (1976), cited in Barry and Hardin (1982, p. 234).

votes. While appearing as a neat formal solution to cycles and manipulation in voting procedures, it has the disadvantage of doing away with general participation and consent. It also raises the disquieting (low but existent) possibility that the person selected to decide racial policy might be Adolf Hitler. Most people would be unwilling to accept even an infinitesimal risk of this. Besides, from a participatory point of view, selection by lot would not reflect active majority consent, so the same arguments used against representation could be turned against stochastic democracy.

Taken together, Arrow's conclusions and conditions have posed a dilemma for democratic theorists over the last forty years. They seem to offer a sharp and unpalatable choice: either abandon democracy (as defined by his four conditions) or give up the idea of achieving non-arbitrary and stable collective policies. One crucial question here is how often, using fully democratic Condorcet procedures, one could expect to end up with no unbeatable winner. Assuming that all individual preference orderings are equiprobable, the probability that there is no such winner varies strongly with the number of options being voted on and more weakly with the number of voters. With three alternatives in play and a very large number of voters, one might expect to get a Condorcet winner in over 90 per cent of votes. With eight alternatives and large numbers of voters, one would emerge in just under 60 per cent of cases (Riker, 1982, p. 122).

The main reason why some individual elections and policy votes would produce a Condorcet winner, and others not, lies in the fact that the array of individual preference orderings would differ in each case. Either naturally or artificially, preference orderings might not include those which give rise to cycles. The commonest example is where alternatives can be arrayed along a single dimension (say, from left to right) and diminish in attractiveness to voters the further they are distant (in either direction) from them (the condition known technically as single peaked preference orderings). In such a situation the alternative supported by the median elector at the middle of the distribution will always be the Condorcet winner. If those to the left of this position try to vote it down, it will be supported by all those to the right of it, as it is closer to these voters than is any alternative supported against it by the Left. And for the same reason it will be supported by those to its left whenever attacked by those to its right. Thus it will always attract 50 per cent of the vote plus 1 voter. No other alternative can beat it and the median position emerges as the majority choice with a guaranteed winner (Downs, 1957; Black, 1958). This situation is illustrated in figure 6.1.

This situation can be generalized. Suppose there are a number of issues to be voted on but each is decided separately. We have seen that this is what happens in practice with initiatives and referendums because courts have ruled that each proposal must be voted on separately (chapter 4). It may often make sense to do things in this way because, for example, decisions about river quality have no discernible connection with prison sentencing policy.

Where issues are discussed and decided separately and singly, each

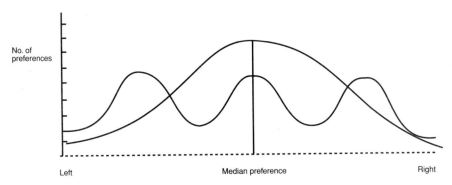

Figure 6.1 How any distribution of single-peaked preferences over one dimension guarantees a stable majority centred on the median

Note: As the median divides the preference distribution evenly, and is always preferred by voters in the one half to any preference of the other half, the median preference will always obtain one-half plus 1 in any vote.

has a winning median position, so there is no problem with cycles (Ordeshook, 1986, p. 250). However, this might still produce a potential paradox. This is illustrated in table 6.4. If the issues are voted on separately, alternative a wins on all issues. But if they were put together, perhaps in the election programme of a political party, the party supporting alternative b on each issue would win overall.

This underlines the general point that decisions about voting procedures will always affect substantive outcomes. The crucial question here is whether it is better to resolve issues separately or together. A relevant point which can be settled (unusually in this context!) by empirical research is how politicians, parties and electors choose to discuss issues when left free to tackle them on their own. The evidence is that in an uncertain and not well understood world the connections between different issue-areas are so tenuous, disputed, uncertain and contingent that they are for the most part considered separately, even by the most sophisticated decision-makers (Laver and Budge, 1992; Klingemann, Hofferbert, Budge et al., 1994; see summary of these results in section 6.3 below).

The voting procedures and paradoxes considered here, however, emerge from the postulate that everyone has fairly complete information and time for calculation of possible interactions. On this basis McLean (1989, pp. 121–4) echoing the general tendencies of the literature, argues that all issues are complex and interrelated; that we choose politically between general states of the nation or of the world

Table 6.4 Party B wins on its overall programme even though a majority opposes its position on each specific issue

	Issues		
Voter	x	y	z
1	a	b	b
2	b	a	b
3	b	b	a
4	a	a	a
5	a	a	a

a and b are different alternatives on each policy, which may be positions endorsed by political parties A and B.

rather than between alternatives in individual issue-areas; and hence all policy-areas are interconnected and must be seen in multidimensional terms. And McKelvey (1979) and Schofield (1985) have shown that in practice cycles are inevitable where more than three policy-dimensions are involved, and highly likely even in two.

Where does this leave the decision between representative and direct democracy? Four main arguments have been put forward to show that the possibility of cycles and manipulation weighs more against direct democracy:

(1)   The first, which underlies some of the other arguments, too, is that politicians are better able and have more opportunity to set up structures and arrangements which reduce the possibility of cycles emerging. A well-known example is Shepsle and Weingast's (1981) analysis of US Congressional procedures. They hypothesized that the concentration of decision-making in Congressional committees forced members to consider just one issue-area (the area of the committee's jurisdiction) at a time. Moreover, voting in the full House is based on committee recommendations and so confined by procedures to one policy-area in turn. This ensures that there will be a Condorcet winner at the median of each single dimension, thus avoiding voting cycles.

Similar institutional constraints, with the same stabilizing effects, might be seen in the organization of Parliamentary regimes into subject-specific Ministries. Parliamentary investigations into the Executive, and bills in the full Chamber, are usually focused on one Ministry and hence upon one policy-area.

The argument then is that voting by representatives is highly structured in this and other ways which avoid cycles and are thus geared to making fixed and authoritative decisions. This is contrasted with the unorganized and unstructured nature of popular voting, which has no way of guarding against cycles. Not only is this a diagnosis which emerges from the debate on formal voting procedures but it is made in a broader and less specific way by students of American popular initiatives such as Magleby (1984) and to a lesser extent Cronin (1989).

We should note parenthetically, however, that the argument has certain weaknesses:
(i)   Committees are set up to serve some interest which wants to have the area separated off. Thus there is no safeguard that the

legislative structure does not build in advantages for some minorities and special interests. But this very possibility is often used as a criticism of popular policy voting.

(ii)   Structure, of course, is not solely an attribute of legislatures. As we have seen, direct voting has been highly structured by judicial decisions so that it too focuses on single issues (and also futher eliminates the possibility of cycles by having only two options to choose from on each proposal). Party participation and endorsement would structure voting procedures even more, as in contemporary legislatures.

(iii)   The argument that it is efficient to separate off single issues runs against other assumptions thought to favour representative democracy and which engender voting problems in the first place. With perfect information and costless calculation McLean argues eloquently that it is irrational to consider issues separately and singly: each general 'state of world' should be considered against each other proposed 'state of the world' – multi-dimensionally. As against that we clearly *do* live in a world with imperfect information, so it does seem efficient to decide issues separately, as political parties do (see section 6.3 below). But in that case we should also worry much less about cycles emerging, and the possibility of them doing so cannot be used as an argument against direct democracy.

(2)   If we stick to the idea of decisions being made with constant reference to other policy-areas, and thus multi-dimensionally and interconnectedly, a further argument can be made in favour of representative handling of issues. Being more sophisticated and on average better informed than ordinary voters, representatives are more likely to engage in strategic voting, that is, stating preferences insincerely, running stalking-horse alternatives, manipulating the sequence of votes etc.

As noted, this is an undesirable quality of a voting procedure in itself. However, in an imperfect world it might make representatives more resistant to manipulation by would-be agenda-setters. Moreover, some formal analyses (e.g. Banks, 1985) conclude that strategic voting avoids cycles better than sincere voting, when issues are being considered together (on the other hand, the example quoted above (Miller, 1993, pp. 79–80) shows that strategic voting can in some cases prevent an otherwise unbeatable alternative emerging as winner in a situation which would otherwise produce one).

In any case, the question of whether there is strategic voting or not depends on party leads. Again, in this argument we have representative voting contrasted with popular voting as though they were quite different and separate things. But, as we have constantly emphasized, parties would influence direct policy-voting as they now influence Parliamentary, so the attempted contrast as to how individuals would react in legislatures and populations is an unrealistic one which ignores the initiating and guiding role of parties in both cases.

(3)   Also ignoring the centrality of parties to both representative and direct democracy, McLean (1989) details the problems of manipulation and cycling listed above. He believes, as noted earlier, that any rational voter will wish to put all the issues together and choose between alternative states of the world. This makes some cycling inevitable under Condorcet procedures, and Borda counts are manipulable in the ways already discussed, as are all other voting procedures. This leads McLean to discount the benefits offered by direct democracy in terms of extending participation and consent, as there is no guarantee that majorities will emerge in the context of collective choice. Indeed, direct democracy might well undermine popular acceptance of the regime: 'If people come to understand cycles, the present legitimacy of elected governments may diminish. New technology [electronic discussion and voting etc.] is more likely to reveal those problems than old' (McLean, 1989, p. 126).

In spite of his clear recognition of the feasibility of direct democracy, McLean is therefore sceptical about its benefits. His general conclusion (implied throughout rather than actually stated), given that direct democracy cannot overcome cycling and manipulability, is that we should muddle along with representative systems – though these can certainly be improved in many ways to give fairer results (1989, pp. 172–3).

This argument rests on the inevitability of voting paradoxes emerging and hence crucially on the assumptions that generate them – such as the idea that choices are between three or more options; that preferences can be ranked but not scored; that all issues must be put together in making a decision about any one of them.

This last assumption particularly assumes a world in which there is a lot of information about connections which voters have time to assimilate (otherwise they might tackle issues one at a time). We shall be contrasting this assumption of near-perfect information with what is revealed in analyses of actual political discussion in section 6.3, and shall only comment here that the political world seems more likely to be characterized by desperate scarcities of information rather than an abundance of easily assimilated facts. If that is indeed the case, the problems of aggregation may well not emerge in actual popular voting, and this particular criticism of it would be rendered irrelevant.

(4)   Before examining this possibility, we should note that Riker (1982) has also used the possibility of cycles to generate even stronger and more pessimistic conclusions. Perhaps even the limited situations in which cycles do not emerge are absent in actual politics, so there is never any median Condorcet winner, and political outcomes are always unstable and in flux. Collective policies in this case are made arbitrarily and contingently and are always liable to displacement by some other set (which, however, politicians may take a long time to find, giving an illusion of stability to the process).

No real popular majorities thus exist for any policy. Given this, the idea that governments should carry out the will of the people is illusory, as there is no (majority) will to carry out – at any rate for one policy-option as opposed to another. The only question on which a genuine majority could emerge is whether the government has performed well or badly. By this route we arrive back at representative democracy. It is the only feasible way of expressing popular choices, but these must be indirect, on men not measures (Liberalism as opposed to Populism in Riker's terminology).

The flaw in this argument, as pointed out in chapter 3, is that electors making judgements about government performance suffer the same difficulties as when making choices of policy-options. That is, if they are asked to choose one out of three or more alternative judgements, cycles will emerge. And this will be the common situation, as judgements must take the form 'Has the Conservative government done better or worse than a Liberal, Christian or Labour one would have done in its place?' This means that governments may well be removed arbitrarily, and if so 'we cannot infer from removal from office that an officeholder's conduct was in fact disapproved of by the voters' (Coleman and Ferejohn, 1986, p. 22).

There are two possible reactions to this. One is to argue that uncertainty about removal from office, even though it may be arbitrary, functions as another check in a system of dispersed powers which prevents tyranny. At many points Riker seems to be making this essentially Madisonian point: limitations and checks are a good thing in themselves and we do not need to bother whether their outcomes reflect majority opinion because none exists.

The other reaction is to argue that judgements about governments are essentially binary: has the government done well or badly? In the American case on which Riker was concentrating, enough negative judgements of this sort mean automatically that the other party would get in. Which opposition party would benefit under a multi-party system is unclear, but Riker could argue this is unimportant: what is important is to decide if the incumbents stay in or not.

If there are only two options, there are no cycles. It was perhaps in this sense that Riker meant to say there could be a genuinely majority judgement about government but not about policy. The problem for his argument here is that one could, no more arbitrarily, restrict policy choices to two options, as current popular initiatives in Switzerland and elsewhere actually do. In this case genuine popular majorities would emerge on policies, so the whole argument for confining voting to representative elections collapses.

6.3 The Structure of Political Debate

Riker's is the extreme example of a pessimistic strain in the formal literature, which discounts the possibility of democracy because voting procedures cannot guarantee the emergence of a true majority. Note that although the argument has been turned against direct democracy it applies to representative democracy just as much.

One might have thought that even on its own assumptions and in its own terms, the critique would not automatically lead to such extreme conclusions. One might settle for an over 90 per cent probability of a popular majority emerging over three options (McLean, 1989, p. 123). One would not know which specific votes represented a true majority, of course. But we are perfectly willing to take similar chances of finding a truly representative group by random sampling, in scientific experiments and opinion-polling. We might be just as willing to accept procedures which gave a guarantee that true majorities would emerge on most votes and accept all of the results, knowing that a small minority are flawed. In an uncertain world we pursue probabilistic courses of action like this all the time.

Of course, there is always the additional possibility of strategic voting and manipulation. But this does not necessarily undermine the possibility of ever finding a real majority, since as noted in some multi-issue situations it may actually enhance the possibility of a stable majority emerging.

The prospects of stable majorities may also be enhanced by institutional arrangements. We have already pointed to the universal practice of offering only two alternatives on each initiative proposal – some change versus the status quo. This restriction on the number of options automatically produces a majority for one side or the other. It does favour the status quo but not necessarily one type of political interest (chapter 4 above). So it cannot be seen as arbitrary in a narrowly political sense. Moreover some decisions, like whether to impose the death penalty or not, seem naturally dichotomous. The courts have also restricted initiative proposals to one issue at a time, thus favouring the emergence of a unidimensional range of alternatives with a median winner.

It is true that deciding on issues one by one may produce different results from deciding them all together, and to this extent may arbitrarily favour certain outcomes over others (cf. table 6.4 above). On this point at any rate a party-based direct democracy may actually avoid arbitrariness better than a party-based representative democracy. The latter has only general elections in which electors choose parties on the basis of an overall policy-package (possibly among other criteria like competence and record). Though they may disagree with elements in this package, they have no possibility of reconsidering them, as most issues fade out before the next election.

In a party-based direct democracy, electors can also choose alternative governments on the basis of their policy package. Sooner or later, depending on the moratorium allowed the government to implement its programmes, they have the opportunity to vote on individual elements in the package, in the light of experience and reflection. If overall the package has been successful, they may well change their minds on the elements they had initially opposed. If, on the other hand, it has had bad effects, they can vote it down. Party policy-packages are generally so loosely structured that dropping one element will in most cases have little effect on the rest.

This possibility raises three points:

(1) Much of the formal discussion of voting procedures rests on the idea that there is only one vote on an issue, which takes place at a particular point in time and settles the matter. Immediately we allow for a continuous process of evaluation and repeated voting (favoured by the procedures of direct democracy (cf. Barber, 1984)), some negative consequences of paradoxes can be ameliorated if not totally evaded. Changing decisions can from one point of view be regarded

as destabilizing: but if policies are regarded as bad by a majority of electors after experience of their effects, should they not be changed? Rigidity is not necessarily a virtue.

(2)   This point ties in with Miller's (1993) discussion of deliberative voting (see also Fishkin, 1993). The process of reaching a decision is envisaged as an 'open and uncoerced discussion of the issue at stake with the aim of arriving at an agreed judgement . . . a process whereby initial preferences are transformed to take account of the views of others (Miller, 1993, p. 75). Miller argues that this involves reasoned argument, defending interests by references to general principles which cover other interests too. This fosters a wider and more inclusive view, which may involve moderating the claims of my own group to meet those of others, under the same principles.

This is quite a different view of the process of decision-making from the classical liberal one whereby individual preferences are fixed and the problem lies simply in aggregating them – the view which underlies many of the aggregation problems presented in the preceding section. Deliberation would probably eliminate many extreme preference orderings and thus make it likely that cycles could be avoided and true majorities found. By helping discussants arrive at a broadly similar view of the situation it may also help to make preferences single-peaked and to place them on an underlying continuum which also guarantees a majority round the median.

There are obvious parallels here with Fishkin's ideas and in a broader sense with those of participation theorists like Barber (1984) and Pateman (1970). None of these has related the idea of deliberative agreement quite so closely to formal voting theory. However, the general idea that more extended discussion will bring together overall views of the situation, and foster agreement, is common to all although expressed in different ways. The point of view all share is that preferences are not regarded as inherently antagonistic and debate and discussion are considered as having effects beyond the mere statement of opposing views.

Such positions are often asserted by participation theorists as acts of faith, though there is increasing evidence for them, as ideas like televised citizen juries or Fishkin's deliberative polling are actually tried out. (For reports of experiments see the *Independent*, London, 9 May and 19 November 1994.) They also receive considerable support from detailed analyses of practical political debate carried through in the last fifteen years. These provide independent evidence on how mass political discussions actually proceed, and thus about which assumptions – those which generate procedural paradoxes or those which evade them – in fact apply.

(3) It is the basic nature of political debate which is the third point to be considered here, in relation to the possibility that voting may not have the hard-edged, once and for all, strictly antagonistic quality which classic liberals attribute to it. Discussion is focused on how political parties structure debate because it is inevitable that they will have the initiating and guiding role in modern democracies, whether or not these are in formal terms representative or direct.

Information on this, of an amplitude that would have been inconceivable ten or fifteen years ago, has now been made available through the work of the Manifesto Research Group (Budge, Robertson and Hearl, 1987; Laver and Budge, 1992; Klingemann, Hofferbert, Budge et al., 1994; Budge, 1994). This has involved collecting all post-war election programmes for all significant political parties in some twenty democracies. These include almost all the democracies in Western Europe, others like Israel and Japan, and all the overseas 'Anglo-Saxon' democracies like the United States and Australia.

Election programmes (i.e. British party manifestos, US party platforms and their equivalents) are the single most important expression of party ideology and policy. They are designed to appeal to voters and thus to win general elections, but they are also more than that. They constitute the only medium-term plans for the whole of society regularly produced by any social organization. As such they have been shown to have a major influence on how governments act – quite naturally, as they are the only guide ministers and others have on what, collectively, to do in office. Their centrality for parties is shown by the extensive debates, often fiercely fought in conferences and conventions, over what should go into the programme. In some countries the documents are delivered to every household; in others they are presented in full through the press and television. Even where less accessible to ordinary voters, as in the UK and US, the press conferences built around them constitute the opening shot in the party election campaign, and the starting-point for television and press discussion of party policies, which it is hoped will influence mass voting decisions.

If anything can, it is these documents which should show the shape practical political debate takes in modern democracies.

The normal view of debate, particularly where political parties are involved, is of a situation where protagonists take up opposed positions on the same issue, and confront each other on it. On this view, if a Conservative for example advocates harder measures on law and order and tougher sentences for criminals, a Labour spokesman should argue for more leniency across the board, buttressing this position with arguments about the greater efficacy of treatment rather than punishment etc. Similarly, when one argues for the nuclear deterrent, the other should oppose it.

This is the confrontational view. In terms of our previous discussion it fits the picture of hard-edged antagonistic preferences unlikely to be modified by discussion. As regards dimensionality, such confrontations might take place on single issues but equally the discussion could contrast opposed positions in a variety of areas and offer electors the kind of multi-dimensional choices which create voting cycles.

In fact, however, confrontation is not a central feature of the election programmes which have been examined – nor, more impressionistically, is it much evident in television debates between parties. When confronted with a damaging point or a popular policy of the other side, party spokespersons are much more likely to change their ground or shift the focus of discussion rather than to argue directly. The reason is simple: if one side mentions a policy position this is because it is thought to be popular and to gain votes for them – therefore it behoves the other side not to confront this and lose votes, but to get to an area where they have the popular policy and the advantage. Right-wing emphases on law and order are likely to be met by the remark that the root causes need to be tackled and this means doing something about social welfare. Public debate thus has the character of two or more sides talking past each other rather than concentrating on one topic of common concern.

This is the saliency theory of political debate. The different saliency given to divergent aspects of the political situation by different parties could well be seen as a recipe for policy incoherence and as encouraging multi-dimensional perspectives calculated to produce voting cycles and instability. It could also seem manipulative, in the sense that the parties seize on topics of advantage to themselves in attempts to influence voters rather than having a full and frank discussion on each topic (Riker, 1993, pp. 8–9; 118–23).

These, however, are initial impressions. We should also consider the positive choices offered by parties' selective emphases. What they are basically doing is to stress different priorities for action in the current political situation. One party says attention and resources should be concentrated on security and order, while another says the focus should be on welfare and peace. Seen in this light the parties are offering a comprehensive choice between policy priorities – perhaps more so than if they highlighted a series of disagreements on particular issues. As we shall see, such a choice can be formulated in left–right terms, with one overall set of policy-priorities opposed to another. Or it could be made on a number of separate issue-dimensions, in terms of which party is closest to my own position: these distances could then be aggregated to arrive at an overall party choice.

We shall go into the details of this later. In general, however, we should note that if parties and voters decide in terms of priorities between issues rather than sharply opposed preferences on them, the potential for acute disagreement is reduced. Someone who voted for giving welfare first priority is not necessarily opposed to higher defence expenditure if the other party wins: (s)he may indeed think it a good thing in itself, though of lesser importance. Nor are priorities necessarily opposed to each other in the sense that higher defence spending means less for welfare. Both can be kept up by increasing taxes, borrowing, international subsidies, economic expansion etc.

Why should we adopt this saliency theory of debate as opposed to a directly confrontational theory? A conclusive argument is found in the fact that if we want to analyse the full text of election pro-grammes we *have* to take a saliency view. This is because it alone allows full coding of these texts. In them, references to other parties, let alone to their policies, are very limited – under 10 per cent on average and at the level of 1 or 2 per cent of the sentences in many. There are also few endorsements of specific policy-positions or of pledges of specific action except in peripheral areas. There is therefore no real material from which to build policy confrontations in these documents – which are pre-eminently, in their electoral and cam-paigning setting, where one would expect to find them. Instead, we find varying amounts of space devoted to the history and effects of a problem, with possibly references to what the party has done in the past but rarely any precise indication of what it will do in the future.

Nevertheless, the varying length of such discussions signals concern and indicates the priority which in the party's view should be given to problems. To capture this, the scheme developed for comparative coding of over 1,000 programmes from twenty countries counts the sentences of the documents into one of fifty-four categories covering the full range of policy-areas. When percentaged, these scores represent the different emphases (and implicitly, priorities) which parties give to different areas, such as welfare, law and order, or defence. These can then be subjected to statistical analyses designed, among other things, to identify the major dimension(s) of party conflict. An example of the scheme and of the party contrasts which can emerge is given in the accompanying list of coding categories.

Categories used to code sentences in post-war party electoral programmes for twenty countries

101 Foreign Special Relationships: positive
102 Foreign Special Relationships: negative
103 Anti-imperialism
104 Military: positive
105 Military: negative
106 Peace
107 Internationalism: positive
108 European Union: positive
109 Internationalism: negative
110 European Union: negative
201 Freedom and Human Rights
202 Democracy
203 Constitutionalism: positive
204 Constitutionalism: negative
301 Decentralization
302 Centralization
303 Governmental and Administrative Efficiency
304 Political Corruption
305 Political Authority
401 Free Enterprise
402 Incentives
403 Market Regulation
404 Economic Planning
405 Corporatism
406 Protectionism: positive
407 Protectionism: negative
408 Economic Goals
409 Keynesian Demand Management

410 Productivity
411 Technology and Infrastructure
412 Controlled Economy
413 Nationalization
414 Economic Orthodoxy
415 Marxist Analysis
416 Anti-Growth Economy
501 Environmental Protection
502 Culture
503 Social Justice
504 Welfare State Expansion
505 Welfare State Limitation
506 Education Expansion
507 Education Limitation
601 National Way of Life: positive
602 National Way of Life: negative
603 Traditional Morality: positive
604 Traditional Morality: negative
605 Law and Order
606 Social Harmony
607 Multiculturalism: positive
608 Multiculturalism: negative
701 Labour Groups: positive
702 Labour Groups: negative
703 Agriculture
704 Middle-class and Professional Groups
705 Minority Groups
706 Non-economic Demographic Groups

As a result of counting sentences (the natural sense unit of the documents) into these categories, we can confirm that different types of parties do indeed emphasize different policy-areas to a very different extent, thus upholding the saliency theory (Budge, Robertson and Hearl, 1987, pp. 20–35).

On the basis of these counts, however, we can go further, to see whether discussion proceeds along one or many policy continua – whether in other words it is one or multi-dimensional. In this way we can answer some of the basic questions raised before, about the extent to which voting based on this type of political debate is likely to generate cycles or to promote arbitrariness or not.

The 'real' dimensionality of party and electoral spaces has been a matter of extensive discussion both theoretically and empirically. We have seen it looms large because voting cycles are inevitable in Euclidean spaces of three dimensions and above, very likely in spaces of two dimensions, and only to be avoided in spaces of one dimension with single-peaked preferences. It is thus very important to know if the preferences expressed in discussion are one-dimensional in this sense or if they spread over many dimensions.

Much of the earlier debate was conducted in terms of what is the 'true' dimensionality of preferences. In light of our research into party programmes, this question seems misplaced in the sense that a 'true' representation of party positions probably does not exist; and in any case we would not know it when we had it. The propriety of a representation depends primarily on what aspects of party behaviour we want to represent. If it involves a general choice between parties, it seems likely that the most relevant space within which to represent policy positions is a left–right continuum which satisfies the single-peakedness condition. An example, which plots British parties' policy-movements over the post-war period, is given in figure 6.2.

Both parties and media tend to present party positions in election campaigns in terms of the positions shown in this dimension, partly because there is an inevitable element of simplification in public presentation which pushes discussion into it. Moreover, intellectual and international influences all combine to locate discussion on the only policy-dimension which is generalizable across countries, the left–right one. There is strong evidence for this in the fact that statistical analyses aimed at finding communalities between specific issue emphases (factor-analyses) come up for all the party programmes from twenty countries with this as the leading and only common dimension (Budge, Robertson and Hearl, 1987; Laver and Budge, 1992, pp. 25–35).

What are 'Left' and 'Right' in party programmatic terms? The right end [of the continuum] was constructed by adding together [percentages for] references to 'Capitalist economics', 'Social Conservation', 'Freedom and Domestic human rights', and 'Military: positive'. The left end was constructed by adding together [percentages for] 'State intervention', 'Peace and cooperation', 'Democracy', 'Social Services: positive', 'Education: positive' and 'Labour groups: positive'. The final left–right [position] was computed as the total proportion of the [programme] devoted to right-wing references minus the total proportion devoted to left-wing references. (Laver and Budge, 1992, p. 27)

As we have said, this left–right space is the one parties use to position themselves at elections. Figure 6.2 in fact gives a very good picture of the way British parties have evolved over the post-war period, with Conservatives moving very far left to accept the welfare state in the 1950s, both parties coming close in the 1960s on a 'Social Democratic Consensus', and the Conservatives then moving far to the right during the Thatcherite 1980s.

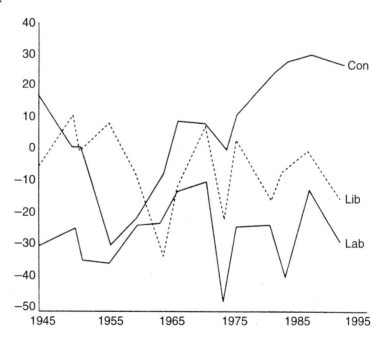

Figure 6.2 Left–right positions of principal British parties, 1945–1992, mapped from their election programmes

However, when it comes to government, the evidence is that parties disaggregate this general position and make decisions in each separate policy-area which are only loosely related to each other. Proof of this comes from further analyses which have related parties' policy emphases to government expenditures. Only in a few countries do general left–right positions influence general expenditure. Mostly, it is emphases on the *specific* policy area (defence, welfare, transport etc.) which relate to expenditures in that area (Klingemann, Hofferbert, Budge et al., 1994). Of course, as we have seen, specific emphases are not unrelated to a general left–right stance. But overall policy is effected through discrete decisions in various policy-areas rather than all at once.

Why should governments make decisions in such a disjointed way, rather than considering the whole state of the world at once, as McLean for one (1989, p. 124) assumes they must do to be rational? Such a conception of rationality assumes that decision-makers are God, with total knowledge and information about all the determinants and consequences of their decisions. We do not live in a world of unlimited full information, and if we did we might not recognize that we had it and would be overwhelmed by the costs of processing it. Attempts to operate on the basis that we know everything of relevance to a decision reached their culmination in Soviet central planning of the post-war period. Its colossal mistakes have been well criticized by Popper (1974) while the 'Science of Muddling Through' with incremental decisions in different policy areas has been eloquently defended by Lindblom (1959).

Discrete, incremental decision-making (Piecemeal Social Engineering in Popper's well-known characterization) seems therefore much better adapted to the actual world of radical information scarcity in which we live. We do not generally know the impact of defence decisions on welfare, economy or environment to take one case, so it is rational to make them separately – a course of action governments are generally pushed into anyway by institutional constraints such as Ministries, and competing interests and personal ambitions as between Ministers.

If governments decide in this way it is even more likely that electors will. This is for two reasons. On average they will have even less inkling of possible interconnections between policy-areas than governments. Secondly, the bodies charged with supervision of popular consultations are likely to insist on issue-questions being voted on separately, as the courts do in practically all cases at the present time. These constraints seem perfectly rational in light of the points made above. Incidentally, the argument also indicates that in case of conflict between the majorities on specific issues and an overall programmatic majority (cf. table 6.4) it would be better to decide discretely on specific policies if one has to make the choice. This is because there is no logical or compellingly rational reason to group separate issue-areas together, as we do not know what are the real connections between them.

Separable issue-areas without interconnections can be conceived of as a series of discrete single dimensions. If electors locate themselves on these dimensions with single-peaked policy preferences, genuine and stable majorities can be found for the position favoured by the median elector (figure 6.1).

A determinate and fair outcome is also more likely since electors in the mass are less likely to engage in strategic voting against the median (cf. the example given by Miller, 1993, where supporters of coal might vote against gas, even though they favour it over nuclear power, in order to promote coal's chances). Problems of organization and co-ordination among a mass electorate make it less likely that such tactics would be pursued in that context than in a committee. Political parties, which alone could achieve such a result, could be banned legally from urging strategic voting to electors. (And our evidence from Switzerland indicates that electors are in any case less likely to follow party leads when they step outside normal policy.)

The theoretical problems raised in this and the preceding section are so complex that by this point one is in danger of missing the wood for the trees. The major conclusion which emerges clearly from the specific arguments is that difficulties in aggregating individual preferences into collective choices in a fair and stable way are exaggerated so far as the normal functioning of democracy is concerned. Preferences are formed and voted on in ways which evade cycles. This is particularly due to the fact that preferences between governments form in a single-dimensional, left–right policy-space, while specific issues are considered inside separable, single dimensions. In both cases stable majorities can form round the position of the median voter.

Decision-making on the basis of single issues in separable dimensions derives in the first instance from the lack of reliable information on connections between issue-areas, or on consequences of one for the other, which leave no alternative to considering them separately.

Formation of an orderly array of single-peaked preferences can be aided by deliberative discussion, whether at first hand or through the televised deliberations of representative samples. Both tendencies can be buttressed in direct democracies by legal requirements to vote on one issue at a time. By requiring a decision between two alternatives on any issue, existing legal rulings in fact guarantee a Condorcet majority, without seeming to restrict choices unduly and without unfairly favouring either Left or Right.

There is thus no evidence that problems in aggregating preferences unduly afflict direct democracy. As is almost the norm in this type of discussion, direct democracy has been criticized for its alleged weaknesses in this regard without subjecting representative democracy to an equally searching analysis. It surely suffers from them as much or more. At bottom, however, the alleged difficulties of finding a stable majority constitute a critique of democracy in any form, since it rests its claim to legitimacy on majority consent and if it cannot produce a majority its major moral prop is knocked away. In fact, no such difficulties arise in democratic practice, since the conditions which generate them do not apply.

6.4 Minorities and Democratic Consent

Majorities may not turn out to be such a problem for democracies but what about minorities? If popular consent is the essence of direct democracy, in what sense can those who voted against winning options be said to have consented to them?

Again, this is a problem for democracy as such rather than just involving direct democracy. Discussions of the effects of popular initiatives in Switzerland and the United States have, however, been particularly sensitive to whether they enforce a 'tyranny of the majority'. The balance of opinion is that they do not, but again few comparisons are made with what goes on elsewhere. On the face of it, representative democracy offers more chances for its 'elective dictatorship' to steamroller legislation through an assembly regardless of the opposition of those who voted against them (or even, in many cases, of those who voted for them).

Perhaps, however, direct democracy does suffer from more of a problem with minority consent. The fact that it emphasizes the need for (continuing) consent more than representative democracy lays it more open to embarrassing questions as to how it can claim to represent the popular will when up to 49 per cent may have voted against the option that is implemented.

A classic answer to this criticism is that democracy – and direct democracy in particular with its extended opportunities for discussion and participation – gives minorities the opportunity first to convince the majority through the force of their ideas (Klingemann, Hofferbert, Budge et al., 1994, show that defeated parties are as likely to influence the agenda in many cases as winning ones). Secondly minorities can try to reverse decisions by lobbying and convincing the majority that they were wrong. Even if they do not succeed, the argument runs, they must support the system which allows them to do this.

At this point, however, it is as well to distinguish between different types of minorities. If we are talking about minorities on one decision, which may in whole or part become part of the majority on the next, the above argument applies fairly well. The rules produce defeat on one question but this is counterbalanced by success on another. In this sense everybody is likely to be in a minority at one point and in a majority in another and are hence likely to accept decisions made by majority voting without too much soul-searching even when they are defeated.

Far different is the position of a cohesive minority regularly set against the majority. The two could be distinguished by ideology (a left-wing minority among a right-wing majority) – but in this case voting separately on specific issues is likely to ameliorate the situation for them, since they can win on individual questions, as they have done in Switzerland and Italy. A more serious problem is where the minority is distinguished by colour, religion or race and defeated over a range of issues which may be vitally important for them.

In the end, the only truly democratic solution may be to allow such a minority to decide issues for itself, either through territorial seces-sion or a functional devolution of decision-making on issues which particularly affect it. We shall consider this case at the end of the section. Without downplaying the seriousness of this question, we shall concern ourselves mostly in the first half of the discussion with the other kind of non-fixed minority. This still raises questions of concern. Some of the considerations that apply to shifting minorities apply to other kinds of minority as well, so the discussion which follows does have more general bearings.

(1) A first set of conditions which eases the sharpness of the contrast between majorities and minorities comes from points made

in the previous discussion on radical scarcities of information and the resulting uncertainties about connections and consequences which follow from it. We have already noted that these make it rational to decide on each issue-area without much reference to others. This does not ensure, but certainly makes more probable, a shift in the composition of minorities and majorities on each issue. Even in the case of more permanent minorities, a series of decisions on specific issues gives more chance to shift the majority on some questions than does a once and for all general election where a government is then given a mandate to go ahead with a range of policies for 3–5 years.

There are, however, other consequences of information scarcity than just the way issues are voted upon. In general, since nobody can foresee with any exactness the full ramifications of a decision or even in many cases its immediate results, the effect must be to diminish the intensity and passion with which both majorities and minorities espouse policies. Far from reducing crime, severe prison regimes may actually produce fitter criminals. The experimental evidence of a deliberative poll not only shows that such considerations change the minority into a majority supporting shorter sentences but undermines the dogmatic nature of discussion in other areas (*Independent*, 9 May 1994).

From a recognition of the complexity and uncertainty inherent in politics, which deliberative discussion certainly fosters but which is inherent in the nature of modern politics itself, policy minorities may well accept temporary defeats philosophically, as it is not inconceivable that the results they want may emerge from the majority decision anyway. In this sense, characteristics of the mass electorate often attacked by representative theorists like Sartori, such as greater uncertainty and ignorance, may actually contribute to the calming of tensions between the majority and the minority (Marcus and Hanson, 1993, pp. 13–15, 147–72). One would not wish to push this argument too far, however. Recognizing the complexity and confusion of the political world may represent a level of sophistication which ideologues (more likely to be activists and politicians) in fact lack.

(2)   This acceptance of the possible correctness of the majority decision is not unlike arguments of Rousseau (1762/1973) about minorities recognizing themselves to be mistaken and accepting the majority view once the vote is taken. Condorcet (1785) even developed this theme in mathematical terms to show that the majority will necessari-

ly make the correct decision if the average citizen is more often right than wrong on the matter under discussion. It does not matter if some or even many are mistaken, provided that the overall average is pulled up by the competence of some in the electorate.

In this sense the minority would do well to accept majority decisions since the fact that they *are* majority decisions guarantees their correctness. Did we operate in a world where there were objectively correct decisions to be made, this would be a highly reassuring argument for the direct democrat. As I have already argued, however, politics are so complex and uncertain that objectively correct decisions to problems rarely exist and where they do we probably do not recognize them. Thus an essential premise behind Condorcet's proof fails.

The other premise, however, has a broader logic. Even in an uncertain world we can surely trust the average person to be more likely to pick better rather than worse options in a modest majority of cases. (For extensive survey evidence that this is indeed so for overall distributions of public opinion, see Page and Shapiro, 1993.) Following Condorcet's reasoning, this guarantees majority choice of the better alternatives in decision-making and constitutes an argument for those in the minority accepting the majority decision on the grounds that it is in some relevant sense better than their own option.

(3)   In an uncertain and divided world of course one can still ask, 'better in what sense?' (information, results in terms of foreseen consequences or unforeseen consequences?) and 'better for whom'? As interests often clash and some groups are disadvantaged by decisions while others benefit, are majority decisions better for the majority but not for the minority?

One relevant consideration here, drawing from our discussion of the nature of political debate, is that many political decisions are about priorities. Political parties are usually preoccupied with urging one priority above another, often in expenditure terms. Neither they nor their supporters necessarily disapprove of priorities further down their order; it is just that others are considered more important.

Condorcet's reasoning seems more applicable to decisions between such priorities for political action, since they involve more of a cognitive and technical element than does direct confrontation between two incompatible alternatives. Those in a minority may well accept the priority voted by the majority – which they accept as valid in itself – even though they considered another more important to act on immediately. They might even accept the majority was more likely to be right in this sense since by definition it embodies a greater range of experience and judgement than the minority.

With Condorcet's proofs we have returned to formal collective choice theory, which as this example shows is not necessarily opposed to popular decision-making although that is the main message that has been taken from it. Beside the idea that minority interests might in some cases be served by more informed majority choices, such a theory offers alternative voting procedures which may meet minority preferences better than finding a straight majority winner.

This, it will be remembered, is the characteristic of Condorcet voting, when the alternative with most first preferences in a series of binary confrontations with the other alternatives is the winner. In contrast the Borda count scores each option according to the place it holds in individual rankings, so the lowest option gets zero points, the one above it $0 + 1$, then $0 + 2$ etc. The winning alternative is the one that gets most points overall, reflecting in this way the distribution of lower-ranking preferences as well as first preferences.

McLean (1989, p. 55) argues that finding a majority winner is at the heart of democracy and thus Condorcet's procedure is to be preferred to Borda's. However, it could also be argued that democracy aims to adopt policies with the maximum possible amount of popular consent and for this reason sizeable minorities and also second preferences ought to be counted. Where a large minority puts the majority's second preference first, there is surely some case for that preference being adopted to maximize consent. In any case, that is clearly a different situation from one where majority and minority totally reverse each other's orderings. There is a case to be made for a procedure which recognizes and reflects this difference and seeks to please everyone rather than as many people as possible (Dummett, 1984, p. 142).

Miller (1993, pp. 87–8) argues that Condorcet is best suited for some situations and Borda for others. Some situations demand clear majority decision while in others general satisfaction and the widest spread of consent should be obtained. This is perhaps most true on distributive issues as opposed to decisions of principle.

As already indicated, parties generally approach politics in terms of priorities for action rather than direct confrontation between two alternatives in the same area. This suggests that Borda counts, with their avoidance of cycles, are the most suitable voting procedure, in principle, for most democratic votes. If voting procedures were to be alternated in a direct democracy, a variety of bodies from Constitutional Courts to Parliaments, to inter-party conferences, to the whole electorate (votes on votes) might decide which procedure was appropriate under particular circumstances. The important point here is that decisions would rest on minority as well as majority consent, and indeed that the very idea of set majorities as opposed to determinate minorities would dissolve away.

The disadvantage of the Borda count in its classic form is that it is open to manipulation, particularly through the use of stalking-horse alternatives which when withdrawn before the vote affect the rank-ordering of other preferences and may result in the most popular being defeated. It also ignores the intensity of preferences – a feature which is likely to affect permanent minorities badly, as they tend to feel more deeply about the matters that touch upon their position.

Both these problems could be solved in a way which would strengthen the position of minorities under the procedure, if we could assign numeric scores to alternatives and add these up rather than using rank-orderings based on the assumption that the intervals between ranks are all equal.

What kind of scoring system for alternatives might be used? A relevant system was uncovered by Kelley and Mirer (1974) in regard to electors' votes in US Presidential elections. These could be related to the balance of likes over dislikes of parties and candidates expressed in reply to a series of survey questions. What electors seemed implictly to do was to add the numbers of likes and dislikes they had for each candidate, sum these, and vote for the candidate with the highest number of likes over dislikes.

This process gave a range of scores from -6 to $+6$, so the end result could be expressed on a 'ladder' of thirteen places on a voting schedule, one ladder for each alternative being voted on. Instead of rank-orderings being arbitrarily used as numbers as in classical Borda counts, placements on ladders could be used to form genuinely numeric scores.

Such a change would benefit minorities in two ways:

1 It would allow them to express the intensity of their feelings, giving the same liberty to the majority if they wished. Minorities however usually feel more intensely than the majority on the matters on which they are a minority, and such a procedure would allow them, as against an indifferent majority, to influence outcomes more

strongly (because their scores would be greater and would thus weigh more heavily in the final aggregation).

2 It would guard against attempts at manipulation by inserting irrelevant alternatives and withdrawing them at the last moment (cf. table 6.1 for how this affects classic Borda counts). As each alternative is assessed on its own and generates its own score, this is unaffected by what happens with other alternatives. As noted earlier, voters in the mass are also likely to assign scores that reflect their true feelings, unless urged to engage in strategic misrepresentation by political parties. But these can, if necessary, be legally forbidden to do so.

The assignment of numbers rather than rank-orderings to preferences is usually criticized on two grounds. First, that there is no generally acceptable public scoring system for doing so (money is usually suggested as the only possible one but is then rejected on the grounds of fairness given at the outset of section 6.2). However, the scoring system suggested here seems fair enough: similar procedures are used in psychological tests and opinion polls with results which are widely accepted. The second objection is on the grounds that subjective preferences are not comparable. We cannot know whether one person's dislikes are the same as another's and therefore whether they should score the same. The point has been made that in everyday life outside welfare economics we make such 'inter-subjective comparisons of utility' all the time, in deciding, for example, whether one child's need for new shoes is greater than another's for a scarf (Barry, 1965, pp. 44–7). Here we need only point out that by assuming equal intervals between rank-order positions, the classic Borda count makes just as strong an assumption – namely that everyone's preferences have the same intensity. We cannot, in other words, rank preferences without making some inter-subjective judgements. Assuming equal intensities is as much an inter-subjective comparison as scoring individual likes and dislikes.

Whatever the final merits of this particular suggestion, the example shows that Borda counts can be based on numeric scores which will go some way to meeting complaints by minorities that their dearest values are trampled on without consideration under purely majoritarian voting procedures. The best way of representing such intensities will demand extensive research and experimentation but there is no doubt that it is practicable along the lines described above.

Taking intensities into account is a way of conciliating minorities without undermining the final power of the majority to determine decisions. For intense minorities can only be decisive where majorities, or most individuals in them, feel relatively indifferent to the choices being made. In such a case it seems legitimate for minorities to be allowed to express their feelings in voting as well as in the form of pressure-group activity, persuasion, demonstrations and all the other ways which are open to them in any democracy. By offering more chance for deliberative discussion and participation in actual decision-making, direct democracy probably has advantages for them here as well.

In considering the intensity of preferences we are moving discussion away from a focus on shifting minorities to the question of persons who are in a relatively fixed minority over a whole range of questions. As remarked before, such minorities are often marked out by class, racial or religious differences, which have caused them to be discriminated against in the past, if not now. They are likely to share preferences over a range of issues as their social position – usually disadvantaged – gives them a common interest and outlook.

Such groups are unlikely to feel their interests are being taken into consideration by the majority or that decisions taken against their opposition are likely to turn out best in the long run. Political complexity and the uncertain consequences of policies are more likely to alienate and anger them (because they do not work for *them*) than to win them over to majority-based decisions.

Under representative democracy, groups like these have formed or allied to a political party and pressure groups, using one of the few resources available to them, their votes (Dahl, 1960, pp. 33ff; Lipset and Rokkan, 1967, pp. 1–67). This course is obviously still open to them under direct democracy, especially one using decision procedures like the modified Borda count which give more weight to minority preferences.

The success of action through a political party and political groups is obviously dependent on circumstances, however, and cannot be guaranteed. While some minorities, above all religious ones, have been successfully accommodated by majority concessions, others feel persistently discriminated against. It is difficult to see such groups as consenting to majority decisions in any but a very formal sense.

In the end, the only satisfactory way of obtaining consent from permanent minorities who always lose on decisions important to them is to offer them the option of secession or devolution, so that at least on these matters they can make decisions for themselves. A territorial minority might well under these circumstances opt to form its own State to take decisions over a whole range of matters, not simply those affecting it directly. Clearly, if minorities do not take up the option of secession left open to them, they are in a deeper and more real sense consenting to the political set-up they find themselves in than where they are not given the option. So offering it very much strengthens the legitimacy of a democracy, above all direct democracies basing themselves on the claim to have continuing consent to their policies. (Dahl, 1989, makes this case very powerfully.)

Offering these options to non-territorial or dispersed minorities is much more difficult, since decision-making cannot be hived off as completely as where separate State institutions can be created in a particular stretch of territory. However, various approximations could be offered as follows:

1   Territorial secession need not involve a physically continuous or contiguous area of land. A whole series of pockets down to the level of individual houses could be put under the jurisdiction of a separate democracy. This is much easier in a modern world marked by economic integration where free trade is increasingly the norm and States have ceased to play the role of separate economic units. Joint physical facilities like roads, water and sewage could be put under common jurisdictions but policing, for example, could be separate. A solution like this has been suggested for Northern Ireland with Nationalists and Unionists each opting for the democracy they would live under (McIver, 1994); and may be evolving slowly and painfully in Palestine.

2   Where even this degree of territorial separation is not feasible, minorities could be offered the possibility of devolution on a personal basis. Individuals could register for self-governing communities with powers over a range of matters, most obviously cultural, but which might include policing and even some economic functions. At the moment, citizens of Brussels can register themselves as either Flemish- or French-speaking, thus putting themselves under an appropriate community council on a personal basis. The most thoroughgoing system of this kind was the Millet system of the Turkish Empire, where each religious community was self-governing under its own head, and the Empire itself had little to do with them but to tax.

3   Other opportunities for minorities to take charge of their own destinies in areas where it matters to them may well occur within the functional associations discussed in the next section. Particular economic sectors for example are often dominated by a particular ethnic

or social group, so any arrangement delegating decision-making to participants in that area has the effect of increasing the autonomy of the minority within it. The general emphasis of direct democracy on the empowerment of individuals and groups within the collectivity, fashionably termed subsidiarity at the present time, should enable minorities to tolerate better the decisions of the larger majority on matters of common concern.

6.5 Political Units for Direct Democracy

The question of permanent minorities and their right to secession brings us inevitably to the question of the proper unit within which direct democracy should function. R. A. Dahl (1974, 1989) has been a pioneer in re-emphasizing this question in the modern context. The questions of territorial and other boundaries, and of the proper size of the political unit, have been inseparably linked to questions of what kind of democracy was desired, since the very beginning of political philosophy. This was prompted in large part by the idea that the unit should be small enough for all citizens to meet face to face, and to a lesser extent by the feeling that it should be small enough and homogeneous enough to generate a 'General Will' (Rousseau, 1762/1973).

The point has been a centrepiece in the arguments of both proponents and critics of popular participation, and has been very effective, as we saw in chapter 1, in dismissing any widespread participation in decision-making as impracticable. If we opt for mediated forms of direct democracy rather than unmediated, and draw on modern inventions like the political party and electronic communication, we cease to be bound by these considerations. This is particularly the case if we accept society as pluralistic and envisage extensive devolution to, and empowerment of, minorities within the unit, as we must do if we take popular consent seriously.

Pluralism and the reality of overlapping political jurisdictions have also to be accepted at the international level. It is no longer feasible, if it ever was, to think of traditional States as hard-shelled entities capable of providing for all the needs of their citizens culturally, spiritually and materially. Such a conception encouraged intolerance internally and aggression abroad. In the post-war world it has become difficult even to think of individual States as providing military security, their traditional function, since ultimate power lies in the hand of international alliances like NATO and their councils and assemblies. Within them the United States may have by far the greatest influence but is also bound by collective decisions in the long run.

We live therefore in a world of overlapping political jurisdictions, both internationally, and internally within existing States. While nothing in our discussion of direct democracy could not apply in principle to any of these units, the entity most in mind because of its continuing influence has been the traditional State. This is because the current erosion of its powers downwards and upwards has still left it the most omni-competent political unit existing at the present time, so it is natural to set the discussion within this context. To take two examples close to the heart of our analysis, both political parties and public electronic networks are predominantly organized on a national basis.

Nevertheless, nothing precludes them operating within sub-State units, as to some extent both do (within Britain in Scotland, and within Scotland in Aberdeen, for example).

There is thus no obstacle in principle to direct democracies being created for the areas in which their populations wish to take control. Whether they set themselves up as communes or municipalities, or regions of existing States, the reality will in any case be one of overlapping jurisdictions. Matters of common concern will have to be agreed with the broader entities to which they belong (not necessarily traditional States but also newer international groupings), with territorial neighbours and with autonomous personal networks and functional organizations cutting across territorial boundaries.

The picture at the international level is the same. With increasingly integrated world markets, democratic State governments become only actors – influential, but only one among many others – in the process of determining economic policy. The same is true of military and foreign policy, as has been noted: and of course of matters like energy and the environment. Even culture and education are increasingly governed by international tendencies spread by world-wide media no longer based within particular countries or controlled by their governments (Held, 1993b, pp. 25–47).

Many of these new international bodies are radically undemocratic, at best influenced by representatives of national governments which operate at several removes from any popular mandate about what they should do. Some of the developing media networks are dictatorial in their internal structure, and markets are often not subject to any political authority. While this may give them advantages of flexibility, markets do depend for their long-term stability on some political support and regulation. Where these are lacking, chaos and disorder may result rather than a flexible world-wide distribution of resources.

Undemocratic or non-democratic arrangements at world level have been used as an argument against improving the quality of democracy at national or sub-national level. Why bother, the argument essentially runs, since most of the important decisions are taken elsewhere, at levels which popular majorities within States cannot affect?

As we have witnessed many examples of incipient democracies being crippled or toppled by external intervention (Hungary in 1956, Nicaragua in the 1980s, for example) clearly this argument has some weight. But it does not lead logically to counsels of despair. Another proper response is to work for democracy and even for direct democracy, at all levels, from the smallest sub-national ones to the largest international groupings. Electronics and parties make it possible to envisage their citizens and members deciding policy, though it is clearly more difficult for them to do so than in the case of traditional territorial units.

At the level of existing States, there are established institutions and procedures to focus on and to control, or change. At continental and world level these are lacking, particularly if we consider the powerful functional organizations like multinational corporations, whose decisions may affect world populations more than territorially based bodies such as the European Union or the United Nations. In the case of functional organizations, there is even a problem of how to define relevant voters: employees certainly, but also shareholders? And major customers? How about those affected by corporation activities such as mining? Where boundaries should be drawn is obviously debatable.

Even at national and sub-national level any attempts at extending policy participation will undoubtedly be incremental and piecemeal. This is even more likely to be the case internationally. States basing themselves on more extended consultation and participation, however, are also more likely to push for greater openness and accountability at international level. It is probable that this would involve in the first place the creation of international law with effective courts to enforce it (Held, 1993b, p. 43, and 1995, part V) and only secondarily the creation of representative democratic bodies on a territorial base. Nevertheless, pressure from changes at State level would push practices at international level in their own direction, so moves to direct democracy anywhere are likely to have a knock-on effect, no longer constrained by considerations of size and scope.

A world of interdependencies and overlapping jurisdictions would clearly limit the operation of direct democracy within any one political unit. The positive side of this reality is that it also gives direct democracies the opportunity to influence other, less democratic entities, since interdependency cuts both ways. The clearest recent example of this was when the ancient direct democracies of the Grey Leagues (the modern Swiss canton of Graubünden) voted limits on heavy lorries passing through their territory on some of the major Alpine passes, thus provoking a major change of transport policy within the European Union and a likely shift from heavy lorries to more environmentally desirable trains. And this happened after Switzerland voted by referendum to stay out of closer relations with the European Union! A clearer illustration of the potential leverage offered by economic interdependency, and of the workings of direct democracy within it, could hardly be found.

7

From Democratic Rhetoric to Direct Reality

7.1 The Contours of a Realistic Debate

Direct democracy represents the best hope of the future for some and a dangerous and unnecessary risk for others. The majority in the middle are confused by argument and counter-argument, and hence prefer a known status quo to uncertain change – just like voters in referendums and initiatives!

It is hardly healthy, however, to keep on as we are purely by default, especially when democratic processes are in a state of continual flux and popular elements intrude more and more into decision-making. We do not have representative democracy in the old sense any more. Polls are accepted as reflecting public opinion better than parliaments. Controversial legislation is subject to direct action by groups claiming to represent public feelings better than representative bodies. The print and electronic media make big issues of such popular manifestations and initiate discussion and debate on their own account. Parliaments and governments are under intense scrutiny and criticized for being out of touch with the publics which elected them.

Under these circumstances it does not seem sufficient, even for those who would uphold traditional forms of representation, to sit tight and make a spectre of popular activism. It is already with us, even though it rarely takes on the exact form which participation theorists would like. We need to know how to react; whether participation should in general be welcomed or discouraged; and, more immediately, how it might be channelled to make some constructive contribution to democratic politics. There are of course those who say it never can make a constructive contribution, outside representative elections. But if so, we need to be convinced that this is really the case. We also need to be informed how to react, since the reality we face is one of increasing policy participation by ordinary people.

It is in light of such growing *de facto* participation that this book hopes to make both a practical and a theoretical contribution. Its aim has been to voice arguments on both sides, giving due weight to *all* the relevant considerations, so often omitted by one side or the other, in order to arrive at a fully reasoned overall judgement. This task is rendered more difficult as the evidence we have on the actual workings of direct democracy is fragmentary and limited. Such as it is, however, it should be studied, and supplemented by the considerations advanced by both sides which survive analytical scrutiny.

As in many academic discussions the arguments are moral and normative as well as factual – and even when factual in form they are often speculative rather than based on any real investigation. Still, even though no final decision can be made in many cases as to which side is objectively right, the full argument can be stated and examined for plausibility, as well as for its conformity to what evidence exists or to what seems a plausible scenario for the working of direct democracy in practice.

It is remarkable how often only one side *is* examined in discussing this question. The book owes its existence in fact to a hunt for more conclusive arguments than the ones commonly used against direct democracy. It ends with the conclusion that most existing discussions are flawed because they concentrate only on what is wrong with direct democracy, as though it had no positive merits on the one hand, and as though representative forms were totally free of the same faults and failings on the other.

To take one example, popular policy consultations are taken as weakening political parties both organizationally and in terms of their programmatic coherence. This assertion is then discussed as though it had nothing to do with the separation of powers or the necessity to negotiate coalitions at the representative level. When the two are put into juxtaposition, however, such institutional factors would seem to have very strong effects. This analysis has indeed tried to bring in both sides of the comparison quite explicitly and not to leave critiques hanging in the air with vague laudatory references to the moderating effects of representative arrangements which are criticized at popular level for producing exactly the same effects.

The example brings in the other way in which this discussion differs from most other treatments of the subject. It actually recognizes the centrality of political parties to politics at the present time! It is clear that classical representative democracy has been so profoundly modified by the operations of political parties that it should properly be regarded as a variant of party democracy, just as any feasible form of direct democracy would also be run by parties. In contrast, most other discussions present representatives as using their own judgements independently to generate compromise – and contrast their maturity and balance with the ill-informed and unorganized masses rushing willy-nilly into ill-considered discussions! This is just to ignore the structures parties impose on debate even when they too are internally democratic (section 5.6 above).

The similarity of the policies actually passed under both sets of arrangements in the American States indicates that representative and direct forms are not perhaps so different as traditional discussions would have us believe. And the main reason why they are not, of course, is the pervasive influence of party. Where parties lead and organize votes, legislators are disciplined into following the party line, not into making independent judgements, while the masses are organized along the same lines for and against the proposal. Of course, some legislators in some situations may defy their party, but this again brings out similarities with electors who may choose to disregard party cues when they think them unjustified.

The fact that politics will be dominated by parties in all likely scenarios renders many of the traditional arguments on both sides of the question irrelevant. The wisdom or otherwise of policies, the alternatives to be decided on, the very way they are debated – all depend much more immediately on the quality of party leadership than on the quality of either citizens or legislators. Of course, in the long run bad followers may throw up bad leaders, though even here the reverse is probably the case. It is also true that legislators are much closer to the leadership, for which they may form a recruitment pool, and are possibly able to influence the party line while it is being formulated. But they do that in their role as party strategists who would exist anyway, whether under representative or direct democracy.

The almost certain predominance of parties under direct democracy will disappoint many advocates of greater mass participation in policy-making. This is because they conceive of participation as a spontaneous upswelling of popular potential and capabilities; a means of self-improvement leading to greater personal autonomy; a final empowerment of citizens in the face of institutions, including parties, which have sought to bypass them and turn them into consumers, both of policies and of goods.

It is significant that participation theorists themselves hardly mention political parties at all and conceive of popular discussion as free from ideological positions or partisan influences. At the extreme therefore some supporters of unmediated direct democracy would reject the idea of a policy debate dominated by parties and hardly consider it worthwhile moving from representative practices to direct democracy in order to get it.

Political parties have many faults which can be countered to some extent by popular involvement, including internal involvement, in ways detailed immediately below. However, it is simply unrealistic to think that democracy could function without groupings resembling political parties. As observed above, even Greek city-states had proto-parties, when we read between the lines of existing accounts (Bonner, 1967). It runs counter to all we know about modern politics to think that mass societies from 100,000 to 1 billion people could have popular direction of policies without being organized through parties. One of the more undesirable features of the present debate is the way in which both supporters and opponents of direct democracy discuss it in terms of its totally unmediated forms. It is no wonder, because of this assumption, that it ends up being rejected by all but a few idealists with unlimited faith in the spontaneous capacity of the common man or woman.

But as argued in chapter 2, talk of citizens making the important decisions that parliaments now do does not mean that they can dispense with the institutions and procedures which parliaments currently use to reach these decisions. Nor does the population need to, in order to attain a greater share in decision-making. Mediating institutions, above all parties, facilitate rather than impede policy decisions and must be recognized as doing that under democracy in whatever form it occurs.

Our recognition of this simple fact undermines many arguments, valid in themselves, but often turned against proposals for extended popular decision-making. One is the very persuasive case urged powerfully by Robert Dahl (1960, pp. 90–5, 310–35; 1970, pp. 40–64) for the political division of labour. Dahl maintains that most people will want to limit their engagement in politics to give themselves time for other, often more enjoyable persuits. They will not want to engage in endless discussion on the varying merits of policy, no matter how important that is; nor partake in complex procedural manoeuvres; nor take time off work for political education.

All these considerations are very germane to the type of formless political assemblies associated with the student movements of the late 1960s, from which Dahl (1970) draws his main examples. Many of them are subverted, however, if we think of discussion as mainly carried by the media in the shape of programmes very like the ones transmitted now with background analysis, coverage of popular juries and samples assembled for representative discussion, panels taking questions and comments from ordinary viewers etc. No more than current legislators need citizens listen to whole debates beyond the point they think relevant to their vote – which may be simply what side one's party endorses or how the characteristics of the issue appear in left–right terms.

In many ways the media have abolished the distinction between debate and entertainment. In a world where current affairs are one of the great mass diversions to which viewers devote a half-hour or an hour each evening as a way of relaxing, the problem in fact may be working one's way through the mass of potential information which is communicated anyway, rather than awaiting rare nuggets which enable one to cast the vote.

Parties do enable citizens to sift through the mass of facts and to narrow down alternatives. One of Dahl's more persuasive questions is why citizens should be expected to do the work for themselves when we have a perfectly good division of labour, with politicians doing most of the detailed sifting out of choices.

The only credible answer to this is that we should continue to take advantage of politicians' expertise, just as we should with other specialists – while never regarding either as infallible, *pace* Sartori (1987). We can nevertheless take advantage of politicians, parties and the political division of labour just as well in direct as in representative democracy, since all will operate along broadly the same lines under both systems.

Another traditional contrast between representative and direct democracy, which the presence of parties destroys, is any idea of greater institutional balance between popular and informed elite elements. Associated with the Madisonian basis of American constitutional arrangements, this is in any case confined only to certain representative democracies. Doctrines of parliamentary sovereignty in the European case argue explicitly for the concentration of powers in the hands of the representative elite and the government supported by them. Parties, however, function in much the same way under all representative systems, and indeed may well have emerged first in the United States because of the need to break down the separation of powers to produce an effective legislative programme.

7.2 Why have Direct Democracy if we have Parties?

The omnipresence of parties also means that institutional benefits like focusing discussion on one issue at a time, so avoiding voting cycles, and effective representation of minority interests, are also guaranteed by direct democracy, at least to the extent that they are under representative forms. These observations, however, may simply fuel another objection to extending direct democracy, more subtle but also more devastating than those considered up to this point. The whole case has been argued on the basis that any functioning direct democracy is bound also to be a party democracy, in the sense of parties functioning as they do now in representative democracies or even extending their activities and strengthening their penetration of society.

However, if both representative systems and direct ones are dominated by parties, what is the point of changing from one to the other? Granted that legislators vote with their parties, are these not already playing their part in setting broad alternatives before the people and translating them reasonably effectively into government policy? Recent studies of the relationship between what parties say in particular policy-areas and what they do have shown a fair correspondence in ten representative democracies (Klingemann, Hofferbert, Budge et al., 1994). Parties are thus already responsive to popular votes and reasonably accountable for carrying through their programmes. So why do we need more complicated arrangements than those which exist for enforcing responsibility in contemporary democracies?

To answer this point one has to go back to the bases of democracy and of democratic political parties themselves. The latter derive their value, in a democratic context, from acting as facilitators for the transformation of popular feelings and opinions into government action. They do this by presenting alternative programmes, records and candidates in elections, allowing citizens to choose between these and even to reject the old in favour of new alternatives if these offer themselves. Parties derive their democratic value from organizing a choice through elections in this way, and from the winner(s) carrying their policy priorities and candidates into government with some degree of popular endorsement.

Parties are central to the functioning of democracy because they are electoral organizations which also function as governments if they generate sufficient support. Their whole rationale and existence is bound up with elections – either with winning the next election or with capitalizing on the results of the last to justify what they are doing.

While basing themselves on majority or plurality endorsement, parties are, however, driven by narrower interests and ideologies not necessarily shared with all their voters, and unlikely to be supported in their entirety by a majority of the population. This is indeed what makes them so valuable as promoters of minority interests, since their ideology will most likely stress these (whether of one minority or several) and their core supporters will be drawn from these group(s). This is not to say that such minorities will generally be small or hidden. However, even if they are as wide as unionized workers these rarely constitute a majority of the population.

In representing minorities, parties will pass legislation and take executive action which favour them. Under representative democracy this general line will have attracted a majority or plurality of votes at the general election. Thus, though the action may favour core supporters more than others, it will benefit and be supported by many others in the electoral majority too. To take obvious examples, a Socialist party voted in with a majority may extend free welfare and health services, which obviously benefit the poorer sections in society but are not exclusive to them and are supported by the majority. Similarly, a right-wing government may be pledged to regenerate the economy by subsidies to businessmen, which obviously benefit them but may have trickle-down effects for others and were included in the election programme on which it got voted in.

Without elections, governing parties would probably not change policies very much; and they would go on benefiting their particular sets of supporters and interests. Only now they would lack popular endorsement and their actions would tend more and more narrowly to benefit their segment of society and cease to provide spillover benefits for others.

Just as was argued in chapter 1, elections are necessary to have other interests taken into account and to provide an endorsement for what government does. The problem is, however, that general elections held once every three or five years, both to choose a government and to endorse a policy programme, are very blunt instruments for enforcing accountability and providing endorsement. No one can be sure whether a party has been elected on the quality of its candidates or of its policies, on the strength of some dramatic last-minute gesture like cutting taxes, or on long-term plans. Nor is it clear one year after the election whether voters still approve the policies which may have attracted them at the election itself – nor indeed which policies out of a complex package did in fact attract them at the time.

This uncertainty is compounded by unpredictable events which can well blow any government off course. Policy failures or lack of fulfilment can always be attributed to crisis or world depressions. The unpredictability of events and uncertainty about causes and effects all contribute to reducing the accountability of governments, since they can always plead that they tried but it was impossible.

Advocates of responsible government are usually very ready to admit these faults. They have always realized that periodic general elections are a very blunt instrument for ensuring that governments are controlled. Their major argument, however, is that it is the only one possible, and a hundred times better than having no accountability at all.

This last point can readily be admitted. The step from having no elections to having genuine electoral competition is undoubtedly the major one on the road to democracy. From then on, governments and parties will tailor their behaviour to the need to conserve or build popular support in the next election, so in this sense periodic representative elections do enforce a continuing responsiveness on the part of parties.

The question of whether such elections are the *only* way to enforce responsiveness is, however, much more debatable, especially in view of the new feasibility of direct discussion and voting. Is it really better to have a loose package of priorities and other commitments voted on once every five years, which the government then more or less follows over the intervening period regardless of how the situation changes? Would it not be better for electors to vote directly on policy matters once they had experienced the consequences of particular policies, which are in any case often unforeseen and unintended by governments? What about desperately important decisions like going to war which were not foreseen at all but which demand resolution? Might it in any case not be better to unravel the loosely connected priorities in an election programme to see which are genuinely preferred by the populace and which they wish to downgrade?

At the present time, discussion and comment substitute for voting on particular policies. These often generate a great volume of criticism and hostile comment which governments are under no obligation to respond to. Though at times they may change policies because of worries about the next general election, in general they can afford to ignore public opinion, especially in the first two or three years of their term. They can safely assume at that point that any worries will be overtaken before the election by other events. When policy-votes could feasibly be organized on these questions, it is disingenuous to argue that we necessarily have to stick with the blunt instrument of infrequent general elections, especially when countries like Switzerland seem to manage very well with such votes. Given current developments, the alternative to sounding out public opinion through these means is to have it expressed, probably dubiously, in demonstrations and direct action, which always carry some threat of violence.

Direct democracy seems to have the positive merit of sensitizing and informing the workings of party government through regular policy-voting. The nub of this argument is that parties, left to themselves, will pursue their ideological goals and the interests of core supporters whether or not they have their own internal democracy. It is in order to control and harness this tendency that we have elections. Infrequent general elections constitute too little of a check on this (very natural) tendency of political parties, so they need supplementing. In modern democracies this is increasingly provided by pressure-group and media campaigns, by direct action and demonstrations. Being without ultimate policy-sanctions except the threat of violence, a sole reliance on such activities is undesirable. They would be unnecessary, or very much more limited, if government actions could be challenged in effective popular debate and changed by popular policy initiatives.

This, to answer the initial question, is how direct party democracy could improve on representative party democracy. Both are organized and guided by parties but there is a greater potential in the former for sensitizing parties in government to the needs and preferences of the population. As Switzerland, Italy and the American States demonstrate, such policy-interventions can play a useful role. But they could be better organized than they are at present. The next section discusses how a direct party democracy would work in practice, within the mass society which characterizes all democracies today.

7.3 How Direct Democracy Could Function

As pointed out in chapter 2 there are many half-way houses between direct and representative democracy. The pure forms represent the two ends of a continuum rather than a sharply opposed dichotomy. The countries used as examples for the working of the popular initiative – Switzerland, Italy and half the American States – are basically representative democracies with some features of direct democracy grafted on (though Switzerland goes further in that direction than any of the others).

It is only realistic therefore to envisage direct democracies retaining some of the institutional features of the representative democracy from which they have evolved. These would include not only parties – which are intrinsic to modern politics – but governments and parliaments too. While party government would function in much the same way as before – with the important exception that it would debate and pass legislation and seek votes of confidence among the population at large – parliament would change into an advisory, investigative and debating committee informing popular discussion and voting, rather than substituting for it. There are many precedents for institutions changing their role in this way, constitutional monarchies being a prime example. Keeping parliament in an advisory role would help to maintain confidence in the system while other changes were taking place.

Other institutions, like the judiciary and bureaucracy, could function much as they do now. Realistically it is unlikely that they could continue with such restricted entry and so aloofly as they do in many countries today. Their aloof style is in part due to government and parliament acting as buffers for them. In direct democracy one would expect them to open up and to be more accountable and responsive to the public. This is likely to be the result of concurrent influences bringing about the same sort of change as that already discussed for political parties (section 5.6). Such change is likely to be promoted by the spread of popular voting, whether or not some kind of elective or recall procedures were introduced for these institutions. These are not essential to direct democracy in the way it has been defined here, but equally they are not repugnant to it.

Some of the major institutional changes associated with direct democracy would take place in the media – newspapers and magazines but above all television or its successor, the interactive computing–communication device already discussed. Change here is necessary because electronic communications would be the main channel for mass debate and voting. Hence, the way in which they were regulated and controlled would be vital for the quality of the democracy.

Regulation might embrace only the party-political aspects of communications networks or it might extend to the full question of control. It is unlikely that all the electronic media would be in State hands but it is likely that regulation would ensure diversity of ownership. This would in any case be enhanced by the increasing number of channels working on a cross-national or even world basis, and by the empowerment of viewers and listeners through technical changes in the two-way computer which will replace present-day TV.

The political aspects of transmission and two-way communication might well be managed by an all-party committee charged to negotiate broadcasting arrangements accepted by all its members; or by a parliamentary commission. Probably this would cover political advertising. Arrangements for group or individual interventions in televised programmes would also need to be vetted. Courts could play a part in these arrangements or hear appeals; they might well assess the wording and form of legislative and executive motions put to the people. Here an advisory parliament could also take a hand, ensuring the fairness of wording and procedures by negotiation among the constituent parties.

The basic point is that no direct democracy, no more than any other democracy, could work in a vacuum. There have to be rules and bodies to regulate procedures for voting and debate, as well as to implement decisions once taken. These have to evolve from the institutions which function under representative democracy. It is a mistake to believe that 'the people' could take care of all this without institutions, just as it is a mistake to think that the latter are incompatible with greater popular empowerment.

These reflections should meet, at any rate to some extent, the widespread unease felt by many democrats about control of the media. A major worry is that the conduct of popular consultations could fall into the hands of some demagogue who would use them to create a populist dictatorship. This fear goes back to Napoleon and his nephew in nineteenth-century France, who both set themselves up on the basis of carefully manipulated popular plebiscites. De Gaulle's use of referendums was less Napoleonic than his style might have indicated, but not devoid of manipulative elements (Bogdanor, 1994, pp. 56–61).

However, it is worth pointing out that the major demagogues of post-war television (Wallace, Perot, Berlusconi) have emerged in representative democracies and in the context of relatively unregulated television networks. The main problem is not regulation itself but ensuring that it is fair and gives equal access to all those concerned with an issue.

Within this set of institutions we could imagine the political cycle proceeding as follows:

(1) There is a general election campaign to elect a government which proceeds more or less as in a representative democracy. During this period no direct policy consultations are held as the competing parties offer general policy programmes for government, just as they do at present. While they may attract votes for other reasons (competence in managing government, candidate appeal etc.), increased support is attracted at least in part by the policies put forward, and regarded as endorsing these policies for action by the government.

While in principle governments could be elected directly, it might be convenient to use the election to select a parliament where parties would have representatives in proportion to the popular votes they attract. This, of course, happens in many representative democracies today; the difference is that parliament would in this case be purely advisory and the government dependent on popular rather than legislative votes of confidence. Parliament, however, could be given many functions corresponding to its original designation as the 'grand jury of the nation'. Obvious ones would be to hold televised debates on topics coming up for a popular vote, possibly drafting the wording of measures to be put to a popular vote, and fleshing in the details of the decisions which are carried. Parliament might also investigate the implementation of policies through specialized committees, and supervise the regulation of the media and channels of general political debate and communication. Many of these functions are performed by legislatures at the present time. The fact that the really acute party battles would now move outside parliament might paradoxically free it to perform these representative tasks better.

(2)   If any one party won a general election with a majority of votes, it could immediately take office as a government and proceed to put its policy programme into practice. In the more common situation where no party wins a majority either one party could form a minority government by agreement with the other parties, or it could negotiate a coalition government of two or more parties. In either case a government programme should be published and popular challenges allowed which might precipitate a vote of confidence. Such procedures would be followed until a government was either not challenged or won the ensuing vote of confidence.

(3)   The government's policy-priorities having received general popular endorsement, it would be reasonable for these to be exempted from challenge, or be made difficult to challenge, for a certain period after a general election – perhaps a year or eighteen months. This would allow for the programme, insofar as it *was* integrated, to be enacted, and the consequences seen and experienced.

It must be said, however, that the policy-priorities listed in election programmes are contingently rather than logically interlinked. Pursuit of any one of them does not entail pursuit of the others in any logical or substantive sense. If individual priorities or policies were open to immediate challenge, this would not impede the others, so how challenges are handled is a matter of procedural choice for each direct democracy to decide on its own.

On the other hand, it makes real sense to allow popular challenges to government policies at *some* point in the inter-election period. Arguments that beneficial effects need a long time to work their way through, so that they should not be challenged in the short term, are usually buttresses for failing policies or for going counter to obvious majority preferences. Given the high levels of political uncertainty and the inadequacies of forecasting, appeals to long-term effects should not be privileged.

(4)   Two types of popular vote could thus take place on policy. One, on policies not covered in a government programme, might take place any time; the other, on policies covered by the programme, outside the restricted period following election. Governments could if they chose make particularly important policies votes of confidence. Adverse majorities on these would bring down the government. New governments could be formed by party negotiations without involving new general elections but involving the possibility of a vote of confidence if their programme were challenged with enough popular

support. If such a governmental programme were unchallenged or won a popular vote, it too could have a period of grace without votes on constituent policies.

(5)   There is a growing contemporary practice for governments themselves to put policies to a popular vote, whether to avoid internal splits or to legitimize the policy more clearly. Governments in direct democracy should certainly be authorized to do this. Following Swiss practice, they might be bound to do so through constitutional provisions to put changes in treaties or constitutions to a referendum.

(6)   What would such popular votes entail in the way of associated political activity? The actual conduct of initiatives promoted outside government, and referendums sponsored by government need not differ much. One would envisage:

(i)   Initial scrutiny of the motion by relevant bodies – courts, legislative commissions or parliament – to establish wording and scope. No serious objections have been raised in the existing literature to the restriction of motions to one policy-area at a time nor to the convention that there should be only two options to vote on, the suggested change versus the status quo. As we have seen, there are good theoretical reasons for sticking to these procedural forms in the absence of convincing objections. Magleby (1994b, p. 98) makes a good case for the wording of questions being simple, general and clear – in contrast to some American States which put a detailed piece of legislation in front of voters. If the wording of a question is very general, its detailed implementation through legislative, bureaucratic or foreign action should also be subject to a right of popular challenge.

(ii)   Decisions about procedural matters would be followed by debate on the measure's substantive merits. If a special organization were dedicated to ensuring fair electronic coverage of policy discussions, this could relay initial debate in parliament, and possibly the proceedings of committees of enquiry on the Swedish model; then go on to party broadcasts, deliberative discussion by representative samples and juries, transmission of local meetings, phone-ins, questions and comments to national media. In other words the whole gamut of current coverage should be systematically organized on a regular basis.

   If a channel were dedicated to such coverage, the other media could treat such discussions as news and provide summaries of the leading events and debates of campaigns in bulletins and current affairs programmes. With such coverage it would be hard to avoid getting some information about the issue, so the problem of information-scarcity bewailed by contemporary analysts might become one of too much redundant information (subject to the objective constraints on knowledge specified in chapter 6). Here party guidance might help greatly in deciding what was relevant and what not.

The most focused and decisive discussions of all might take place in informed groups, but not, given the interactive electronic networks into which everyone would be linked, necessarily face-to-face groups. One could imagine in this relatively unstructured situation that discussion and comment would flow upwards, downwards, sideways and beyond the boundaries of the political unit in which voting would take place. Far from an isolated individual sitting in front of a screen and pressing a button to vote, interactive communication could take place in the office or in the street as well as in the home, and it could link groups as well as individuals.

(iii)   The outcome of all this would be a vote, registered no doubt by pressing a button on the communication device and using an individual voter code number. Voting electronically would remove many obstacles involved in physically turning up to vote at the present time. For example, there need no longer be voting on a number of (unrelated) policy-measures on the same ballot paper, in order to economize on effort.

(iv)   Ease of voting would very likely increase participation beyond present-day levels, even though the less educated and politically ignorant would still disproportionately abstain. No doubt also different areas of policy would attract different levels of voting, depending on their immediacy, interest and technicality. Thus the variation which exists at the present time would not disappear but would be smoothed out. It would be a matter for each individual democracy whether to regard very low turnout as a reason for invalidating the vote. Electronic voting should, however, render such situations less usual.

Would this process of intensive political discussion be too much for the average voter? Most will be recipients of information rather than active contributors, thus disappointing the highest hopes of participation theorists. However, we have noted that informing oneself and deciding on one's position, possibly in consultation with family and friends, is an important aspect of participation in its wider sense (section 1.2). Participation theorists may further console themselves that in absolute terms many more people would debate and discuss policy; and the opportunities to do so would be open in a way they are not today.

In general, worries about voters in direct democracy have been about them having too little information rather than too much. If the balance shifts to them having to take positive action to avoid information rather than acquire it, one can anticipate the generality of voters being better informed. However, individuals have an infinite capacity to shut out unwanted items and no doubt many will do so. Time itself should not be a problem since a single one of the summaries of debates reported on the TV or radio news (watched or heard by a vast majority of the population at some point in the day) should contain more information about the pros and cons of the policy, and of the opposing parties and interests involved, than most people carry to the polls today after whole referendum campaigns.

The entire question of what constitutes sufficient information to cast an intelligent vote is of course a controverted one. It is likely to be more minimal than sophisticated observers have traditionally required. Much of the literature on representative elections contends that the single most important item of information for voting is which party candidates belong to, since this one fact provides a range of indications about past record and ideological views, what interest they are likely to vote for in the future, their likely relationship with you and your groups, etc.

Similarly, a bare bit of information about what alternative on a proposal a party endorses ties policy-positions in with a particular ideology and with the interests which are likely to line up on one side or the other. This is most of what is needed to cast an intelligent vote. It does not take much time to acquire and cannot easily be avoided, given extensive media coverage.

As argued earlier, parties will be strongly motivated to take sides on policy votes where these settle important issues. The price of not doing so would be political irrelevance. The declaration of a party stance gives citizens their essential voting information, painlessly and cheaply.

To say that many voters will get by with this nearly costless minimum is not to deny of course that many others will absorb much more information simply by spending two or three hours in front of the screen as part of their normal relaxation. Nor need this time be spent passively, as two-way communication will make interventions more normal and much easier to carry through. When popular interest is encouraged and planned for rather than ignored, it will increase. It will also express itself through the channels made available rather than at the fringes of legality, through demonstrations and petitions.

The capacity of voters to consider their vote and to absorb information obviously depends on how much is asked of them. How many policy votes would they be required to make in a year, for example? A rough indication is given by the number of important bills the British parliament is asked to pass in a single session – something between twenty and thirty in an average year. Swiss citizens may vote on up to sixteen Federal consultations a year, which as we have seen cover most major policy proposals. (However, there may be equal or double that number of votes at State and local level.)

A fair estimate of the number of policy votes required in a year might thus be about fifty. Where voters have to turn out to polling-stations to register their vote, this might impose burdens and reduce turnout. There is no evidence, however, that Swiss voters suffer from long-term fatigue. Things would be much easier with a direct voting device in every home, or carried on the person, where fifty votes in the year does not seem arduous.

What time costs exist for informing oneself adequately on a vote might in any case be reduced by allocating a certain amount of paid time from work to attend to civic duties. Under representative democracy this is normal for persons serving in local or regional government. There is no reason in principle why it should not be extended to every citizen in a direct democracy, as they all have to vote on policy. There is maternity leave – why not civic leave?

The description given above can only serve as a very minimal sketch of the way a mediated direct democracy would function in the modern world. Hopefully, however, enough of the essentials have been covered to convince the reader that it is practicable and does not involve too much of a break with the past. Certainly the technology is already here. And transferring policy votes to the public from parliament does not go too far beyond existing Swiss practice, which has hardly produced radical or disastrous results.

7.4 Could Citizens Cope?

The aspersions cast by some theorists on the capacity of ordinary people to understand let alone decide policy are matched only by the diffidence of many citizens about their own abilities. The affairs of the nation seem too far removed from day-to-day life, too arcane to be touched by profane hands – especially by those of one's neighbours! Far better that those born to it should take charge and tell us what to do.

These gut feelings are probably the most potent barrier to any greater empowerment of the population, let alone to bringing in a full-blown direct democracy. And defenders of the status quo are very happy to take advantage of them.

As such feelings are instinctive and deeply felt reactions to the very idea of popular decision-making, they are hard to argue with. All we can do here is recapitulate arguments and evidence which demonstrate that citizens in the mass are able to make policy-decisions which are not noticeably worse than those made by legislatures, if not somewhat better.

A first point to be made is that the changes reviewed here are relatively incremental ones. As pointed out in the last section, institutions like parliament would remain and perform many of their traditional tasks, in any realistic scenario.

But above all, the parties and party leaders, though obliged to maintain popular support in ways they can ignore at present, would guide decision-making and take responsibility for its implementation just as they do now. Any feasible form of direct democracy would have to be party democracy. As these would be the same groups and people as direct policy now under the forms of representative democracy, citizens need hardly fear the unknown if they move from parliamentary to popular voting.

What such a change would do is to make parties more responsive to electoral views, not replace parties. On the voting side, evidence from the countries with popular consultation shows that citizens in the mass are politically mature and responsible.

The nature of the literature we have reviewed, which is almost solidly critical of direct democracy and suspicious of popular involvement, has forced on most of this discussion a predominantly defensive tone. Nowhere is this more true than on the question of ordinary people's capacities, which are invariably marked down in the comparison with representatives. Yet where the research has been done (notably in the recent reappraisal of American survey evidence edited by Marcus and Hanson, 1993) it points to notably positive conclusions. Public opinion in the mass is reasonably stable but open to argument, reasonably tolerant, reasonably informed – quite adequate to produce the respectable outcomes which have been shown to emerge from popular voting.

To emphasize the positive merits of the democratic citizenry, one can also bring in – as is rarely done in this debate – the downside of representatives' behaviour in contemporary democracies, and of the actions of political parties unchecked by popular intervention. Without unduly emphasizing the extraordinary trail of sex scandals and petty corruption which British MPs and American congressmen have left behind them, it is difficult to think of major decisions of the last ten or twenty years which popular interventions might not have improved. Popular voting would have protected health and personal services better, safeguarded education and probably done more to protect the environment, if American State and Swiss initiatives are any indication.

Popular voting might also have prevented the self-enrichment of political representatives, whether through straight self-aggrandizement in the United States, government patronage and privatization profits in Britain, or bribes and criminal collusion in Italy. It might also check the tendency of parties to favour their supporters and increasingly their rich backers in the shaping of public policy. The negative redistribution of wealth since the 1980s is a reflection of their influence which a popular majority might oppose. In seeking direct popular support, parties would have to modify these policies in more consensual and constructive ways.

These examples, along with many of the arguments reviewed elsewhere in the book, should encourage democratic citizens to take a fresh look at their own and their neighbours' potential. The experiments with deliberative discussion which have taken place with representative samples of the populace show a maturity and open-mindedness which compare well with that of most legislators.

7.5 The New Challenge of Direct Democracy

Democratization over the last two centuries can be seen as the progressive enfranchisement of larger and larger sections of the population – the middle class, ethnic and religious minorities, workers and women. Enfranchisement gave these groups votes to use in representative elections, which they generally cast in support of a political party which defended their interests against established ones. Enfranchisement thus encouraged dissent and opposition but these were expressed through participation in elections and the community activities which ensuing legislation legalized, rather than in the demonstrations and riots which forced enfranchisement in the first place.

Each successive enlargement provoked resistance and prophecies of doom. The new voters were thought unlikely to pick good representatives; their leaders were adjudged demagogues unsuitable for truly democratic politics; and the parties which were their main political vehicle were condemned as subversive and disruptive.

All this is familiar after going through the debates on direct democracy! Most adults in democratic populations are now enfranchised, so discussion is not focused on new groups being admitted but on existing voters being given extended powers. However, the same doubts about their capacity are expressed as in the past – these are the same worries about the uneducated and ignorant destabilizing democratic processes or a tyrannical majority taking over.

Seeing proposals for direct democracy as simply the latest in a long series of reforms which progressively extended political participation helps give a historical perspective to the arguments analysed here. We can characterize many of them as being habitually made against any broadening of effective participation. This may not be grounds for dismissing them altogether but, when we have checked their pessimistic forecasts against the evidence available, we have not found much that supports them.

The nineteenth- and twentieth-century enfranchisements in fact turned out well. The newer voters behaved responsibly; their leaders stayed within constitutional rules and agreements; their parties competed peacefully with established ones; and the social and other reforms they introduced were moderate, promoted social justice and had a stabilizing effect.

Without enfranchisement there might have been revolution and there would certainly have continued to be unrest and alienation. In the modern period democracy has tended to regenerate itself by extending participation to new groups – the last, very recently in some cases, being women. The continued exclusion of women would not have provoked revolution and fostered only limited unrest. Still, few would now argue as they did in the past that it has in any sense lowered the quality of democracy – on the contrary.

The enfranchisement of women seems the most relevant of the historical analogies to direct democracy. Keeping policy-making within parliaments is not going to provoke a revolution. But it is going to provoke unrest and alienation among groups whose active support is important to democracy and whose participation would invigorate it. It is significant that most of the new issues of the last thirty years have been promoted by demonstrations and direct action, rather than conventional political activities through parties and legislatures. The reasons for this are clear – supporters of these causes feel excluded from decision-making carried on at second hand by representatives who are at best only mildly supportive on the issues. The elective dictatorship of majority parties means that unpopular policies can be enforced years after support for them has evaporated – even without putting them in an electoral programme. This situation is exacerbated with coalition governments which clearly have to make compromises on the programmes endorsed by each of the partners.

In such situations the only actions which can block or promote policies become illegal or semi-legal: strikes, demonstrations, resistance, riots – even terrorism. The people are not inherently anti-democratic. It is just that representative democracies offer them no immediate way to challenge policies other than this. Being able to mount an initiative, or campaign in a referendum, would provide a way of expressing opposition which was constitutional and fully legal, and whose verdict one way or the other would be accepted.

In present-day democracies one can expect direct action and terrorism to increase with increasing frustration about representative processes. Of course, these extra-legal activities often produce valid results. It is also true that representative democracies do offer opportunities for popular opinion to make itself peaceably felt – through polls, petitions, public hearings, media comment and the other channels listed above. However, it is unfortunate that the only way to obtain a decision in many cases is by going beyond these channels.

In this way, extended participation can be seen as a remedy for some of the ills of present-day democracy and as creating opportunities for the inclusion of currently alienated groups, just as successive enfranchisements have done. However, the case for greater popular empowerment is not just based on the need to head off discontent. Much more positively, it can be argued in terms of tapping the new energy and resources which education and social change have created in the community. Can democracies really afford to shut out millions who could contribute so much in the way of information and debate, for all but one day in four or five years? Being reduced to passive recipients of policy prescriptions doled out by often insensitive and unresponsive governments is not the way to build a healthy political or social community. Frustration at not being heard is likely to grow as the channels to carry popular debate are ever more clearly in place.

Direct democracy can therefore be seen as the logical way to modernize our existing regimes. Just as with the nineteenth-century enfranchisements, one can indeed see tentative steps being taken in its direction long before it is officially accepted as the way to go. Governments, in spite of their unwillingness to abandon representative buffers against popular opinion, do defer more to its various expressions. But they stop short of institutionalizing them even when the time seems right to do so.

The very qualities such as extended education and political sophistication which prompt demands for effective popular consultation render democratic populations better able to use their political opportunities responsibly when these are made available to them.

BIBLIOGRAPHY

Aristotle, tr. E. Barker (1958), *Politics* (Oxford, Oxford University Press).

Arrow, Kenneth (1951), *Social Choice and Individual Values* (New York, Wiley).

Arterton, F. C. (1987), *Teledemocracy* (Newbury Park, Calif., Sage).

Banks, Jeffrey, S. (1985), 'Sophisticated Voting Outcomes and Agenda Control', *Social Choice and Welfare*, 4, pp. 295–306.

Barber, Benjamin (1984), *Strong Democracy: Participatory Politics for a New Age* (Berkeley, University of California Press).

Barber, Benjamin (1988), *The Conquest of Politics* (Princeton, NJ, Princeton University Press).

Barry, Brian M. (1965), *Political Argument* (London, Routledge).

Barry, Brian M. and Hardin, R. (1982), *Rational Man and Irrational Society* (Beverly Hills, Sage).

Beetham, David (1993), 'Liberal Democracy and the Limits of Democratization', in Held (1993a), pp. 55–73.

Bell, Daniel (1960), *The End of Ideology* (New York, Random House).

Berelson, B., Lazarsfeld, P. F. and McPhee, W. (1954), *Voting* (Chicago, University of Chicago Press).

Black, D. (1958), *The Theory of Committees and Elections* (Cambridge, Cambridge University Press).

Bogdanor, V. (1991), *Encyclopedia of Political Science* (Oxford, Blackwell).

Bogdanor, V. (1994), 'Western Europe', in Butler and Ranney (1994), pp. 24–97.

Bonner, R. J. (1967), *Aspects of Athenian Democracy* (New York, Russell and Russell; 2nd edn).

Borda, J. D. de (1784), 'Memoire sur les Elections au Scrutin', in *Memoires de l'Academie Royale des Sciences Annee 1781* (Paris, Academie des Sciences).

Budge, Ian (1989), 'L'impatto politico delle technologie informatiche', *Teoria Politica*, 5, pp. 95–110.

Budge, Ian (1990), 'Can Utilitarianism Justify Democracy?', ch. 10 in Lincoln Allison (ed.), *The Utilitarian Response* (London, Sage).

Budge, Ian (1993), 'Rational Choice is More than Economic Theorising', in H. Keman (ed.), *Approaches to Comparative Government* (Amsterdam, Kluwer), pp. 81–101.

Budge, Ian (1994), 'A New Spatial Theory of Party Competition', *British Journal of Political Science*, 24, pp. 443–67.

Budge, Ian and Farlie, D. J. (1977), *Voting and Party Competition* (London, Wiley).

Budge, Ian and Farlie, D. J. (1983), *Explaining and Predicting Elections* (London, Allen and Unwin).

Budge, Ian and Hofferbert, R. (1990), 'Mandates and Policy Outputs: U.S. Party Platforms and Federal Expenditures', *American Political Science Review*, 84, pp. 111–31.

Budge, Ian and Keman, Hans (1990), *Parties and Democracy: Coalition-formation and Government Functioning in Twenty States* (Oxford, Oxford University Press).

Budge, Ian, Robertson, D. and Hearl, D. (eds) (1987), *Ideology, Strategy and Party Change* (Cambridge, Cambridge University Press).

Budge, Ian, Brand, J., Margolis, M. and Smith, A. (1972), *Political Stratification and Democracy* (London, Macmillan).

Butler, David and Ranney, Austin (eds) (1994), *Referendums round the World* (London, Macmillan).

Caciagli, M. and Uleri, P. V. (eds) (1994), *Democrazie e referendum* (Laterza, Rome–Bari).

Coleman, J. and Ferejohn, J. (1986), 'Democracy and Social Choice', *Ethics*, 97, pp. 601–25.

Condorcet, Marquis de (1785), *Essai sur l'application de l'Analyse a la Probabilite des decisions rendues a la Pluralite des voix* (Paris, Imprimerie Royale).

Converse, Philip L. and Pierce, Roy (1986), *Political Representation in France* (Cambridge, Mass., Harvard University Press).

Cronin, Thomas E. (1989), *Direct Democracy: The Politics of Initiative, Referendum and Recall* (Cambridge, Mass., Harvard University Press).

Dahl, R. A. (1956), *A Preface to Democratic Theory* (Chicago: University of Chicago Press).

Dahl, R. A. (1960), *Who Governs?* (New Haven, Yale University Press).

Dahl, R. A. (1970), *Afer the Revolution* (New Haven, Yale University Press).

Dahl, R. A. (1971), *Polyarchy* (New Haven, Yale University Press).

Dahl, R. A. (1985), *A Preface to Economic Democracy* (Berkeley and Los Angeles, University of California Press).

Dahl, R. A. (1989), *Democracy and its Critics* (New Haven, Yale University Press).

Dahl, R. A. and Tufte, E. (1974), *Size and Democracy* (Stanford, Calif., Stanford University Press).

De Winter, Lieven (1992), 'The Belgian Legislator' (Ph.D. Thesis, European University Institute, Florence, Italy).

Downs, A. (1957), *An Economic Theory of Democracy* (New York, Harper).

Dummett, M. (1984), *Voting Procedures* (Oxford, Clarendon Press).

Duverger, M. (1951), *Les partis politiques* (Paris, Colin).

Fishkin, James, S. (1993), *Democracy and Deliberation* (New Haven, Yale University Press).

Franklin, Mark, Mackie, Tom and Valen, Henry (eds) (1992), *Electoral Change* (Cambridge, Cambridge University Press).

Gibbard, A. (1973), 'Manipulation of Voting Schemes', *Econometrica*, 41, pp. 587–601.

Greenstein, F. (1970), *The American Party System and the American People* (Englewood Cliffs, NJ, Prentice-Hall).

Held, David (ed.) (1992), *Prospects for Democracy*, Special Issue of *Political Studies* (Oxford, Blackwell).

Held, David (ed.) (1993a), *Prospects for Democracy: North, South, East, West* (Cambridge, Polity).

Held, David (1993b), 'Democracy: From City States to a Cosmopolitan Order?' in Held (1993a), pp. 13–52.

Held, David (1995), *Democracy and the Global Order* (Cambridge, Polity).

HMSO (1992), *Social Trends 22* (London, HMSO).

Hollander, R. S. (1985), *Video Democracy: The Vote from Home Revolution* (Mount Airy, Md., Lomond).

Jewell, Malcolm E. and Patterson S. C. (1973), *The Legislative Process in the U.S.* (New York, Random House).

Kelley, S. Y. and Mirer, T. (1974), 'The Simple Act of Voting', *American Political Science Review*, 68, pp. 572–91.

Kircheimer, Otto (1966), 'The Transformation of Western European Party Systems', in J. La Palombara and M. Weimer (eds), *Political Parties and Political Development* (Princeton, NJ, Princeton University Press).

Klingemann, H. D., Hofferbert, R., Budge, Ian et al. (1994), *Parties, Policies and Democracy* (Boulder, Colo., Westview).

Knüsel, René and Hottinger, J. T. (1994), 'Regional Movements and Parties in Switzerland', paper presented at European Consortium for Political Research Joint Sessions, Madrid, 1994.

Kobach, K. W. (1994), 'Switzerland', in Butler and Ranney (1994), pp. 98–152.

Kornhauser, A. (1960), *The Politics of Mass Society* (London, Routledge and Kegan Paul).

Kriesi, H. (1994), 'La lunga e complessa vicenda della Confederazione Elvetica', in Caciagli and Uleri (1994), pp. 63–78.

Lagerspetz, E. (forthcoming), 'Paradoxes and Representation', *Electoral Studies*.

Lasswell, H. D. (1941), 'The Garrison State', *American Journal of Sociology*, 46, pp. 132–51.

Laver, M. J. and Budge, Ian (eds) (1992), *Party Policy and Government Coalitions* (London, Macmillan).

Lindblom, C. (1959), 'The Science of Muddling Through', *Public Administration Review*, 19, pp. 79–88.

Linder, W. (1994), *Swiss Democracy* (New York, St Martin's Press).

Lindsay, A. D. (1910), Introduction to J. S. Mill Everyman Edition.

Lipset, S. M., and Rokkan, S. (1967), *Party Systems and Voter Alignments* (New York, Free Press).

McIver, R. (1994), 'A Northern Ireland Peace Plan' (unpublished MS, Department of Government, University of Essex).

McKelvey, R. D. (1979), 'General Conditions for Global Intransitivities in Formal Voting Models', *Econometrica*, 47, pp. 1085–111.

McLean, Iain S. (1987), *Public Choice* (Oxford, Blackwell).

McLean, Iain S. (1989), *Democracy and New Technology* (Cambridge, Polity).

McLean, Iain S. (1991), 'Rational Choice and Politics', *Political Studies*, 39, pp. 496–512.

Madison, James, with Alexander Hamilton and John Jay (1787–8/1911), *The Federalist Papers* (London, Dent).

Magleby, D. B. (1984), *Direct Legislation: Voting on Ballot Propositions in the United States* (Baltimore, Johns Hopkins University Press).

Magleby, D. B. (1994a), 'Direct Legislation in the American States', in Butler and Ranney (1994), pp. 218–54.

Magleby, D. B. (1994b), 'I problematici sviluppi della recente esperienza statunitense', in Caciagli and Uleri (1994), pp. 79–99.

Mair, Peter (1992), 'La trasformazione del partito di massa in Europa', in M. Calise (ed.), *Come cambiano i partiti* (Bologna, Il Mulino), pp. 99–122.

Mansbridge, Jane (1983), *Beyond Adversarial Democracy* (New York, Basic Books).

Marcus, G. E. and Hanson, R. L. (eds) (1993), *Reconsidering the Democratic Public* (University Park, Pa., University of Pennsylvania Press).

Margolis, M. (1978), *Viable Democracy* (London, Penguin).

Margolis, M. and Mauser, G. (eds) (1989), *Manipulating Public Opinion* (Chicago, Dorsey).

Mastropaolo, Alfio (1993), *Il ceto politico* (Rome, La Nuova Italia Scientifica).

Matthews, D. E. (1973), *U.S. Senators and their World* (New York, Norton).

Mill, James (1823), *Essay on Government*, in *Encyclopaedia Britannica*, 2nd edn (Edinburgh 1810–25).

Mill, J. S., Everyman Edition (1910), *Utilitarianism, Liberty, Representative Government*, ed. H. B. Acton (London, Dent).

Miller, David (1993), 'Deliberative Democracy and Social Choice', in Held (1993a), pp. 74–92.

Miller, W. E. and Stokes, D. E. (1963), 'Constituency Influence on Congress', in A. Campbell et al. (eds), *Elections and the Political Order* (New York, Wiley), pp. 351–92.

Möckli, S. (1994), 'Nuove democrazie a confronto', in Caciagli and Uleri (1994), pp. 49–62.

Olson, M. (1965), *The Logic of Collective Action* (Cambridge, Mass., Harvard University Press).

O'Neill, Onora (1990), 'Practices of Toleration', ch. 5 in Judith Lichtenberg (ed.), *Democracy and the Mass Media* (Cambridge, Cambridge University Press).

Ordeshook, Peter (1986), *Game Theory and Political Theory* (Cambridge, Cambridge University Press).

Page, B. I. and Shapiro, R. Y. (1993), 'The Rational Public and Democracy', in Marcus and Hanson (1993), pp. 35–64.

Parekh, Bhiku (1993), 'A Misconceived Discourse on Political Obligation', *Political Studies*, 41, pp. 236–51.

Parry, Geraint (1989), 'Democracy and Amateurism: The Informed Citizen', *Government and Opposition*, 24, pp. 489–502.

Parry, Geraint, Moyser, George and Day, Neil (1992), *Political Participation and Democracy in Britain* (Cambridge, Cambridge University Press).

Pateman, C. (1970), *Participation and Democratic Theory* (Cambridge, Cambridge University Press).

Pierce, Roy (1992), Paper on 'French Representation', presented at Conference on Representation, Wissenschaftzentrum, Berlin.

Plamenatz, John (1973), *Democracy and Illusion* (London, Longman).

Pomper, Gerald (ed.) (1980), *Party Renewal in America* (New York, Praeger).
Popper, Karl (1974), *The Poverty of Historicism* (London, Routledge and Kegan Paul).
Ranney, A. (1994), 'Nuove pratiche e vecchia teoria', in Caciagli and Uleri (1994), pp. 29–48.
Riker, W. H. (1982), *Liberalism against Populism* (San Francisco, Freeman).
Riker, W. H. (ed.) (1993), *Agenda Formation* (Ann Arbor, University of Michigan Press).
Rousseau, J. J., tr. G. D. H. Cole, J. Brumfitt and J. C. Hall (1762/1973), *The Social Contract and Discourses* (London, Dent).
Sartori, Giovanni (1965), *Democratic Theory* (New York, Praeger).
Sartori, Giovanni (1987), *The Theory of Democracy Revisited* (Chatham, NJ, Chatham House Publishers).
Satterthwaite, M. A. (1975), 'Strategy-proofness and Arrow's Conditions', *Journal of Economic Theory*, 10, pp. 187–217.
Schofield, N. (1985), *Social Choice and Democracy* (Berlin, Springer-Verlag).
Schmitter, P. and Lehmbruch, G. (eds) (1979), *Trends towards Corporatist Mediation* (London, Sage).
Schumpeter, Joseph A. (1950), *Capitalism, Socialism and Democracy* (New York, Harper).
Sheeran, M. (1983), *Beyond Majority Rule* (Philadelphia, Religious Society of Friends).
Shepsle, K. and Weingast, B. (1981), 'Structure-induced Equilibrium and Legislative Choice', *Public Choice*, 37, pp. 503–19.
Smout, C. (1984), *A Century of the Scottish People* (London, Fontana).
Tufte, E. (1978), *Political Control of the Economy* (Princeton, NJ, Princeton University Press).
Uleri, P. V. (1994a), 'The Referendum Phenomenon in Italy 1946–1993', paper presented at European Consortium for Political Research Joint Sessions, Madrid, 1994.
Uleri, P. V. (1994b), 'Dall'instaurazione alla crisi democratica', in Caciagli and Uleri (1994), pp. 390–427.
von Beyme, G. (1985), *Political Parties in Western Democracies* (Aldershot, Gower).
Wattenberg, Martin P. (1990), *The Decline of American Political Parties* (Cambridge, Mass., Harvard University Press).
Weale, Albert (forthcoming), *Democracy* (Cambridge, Polity).
Weber, Max (1958), *From Max Weber*, tr. H. H. Gerth and P. C. Wright Mills (New York, Oxford University Press).
Wright, W. E. (ed.) (1971), *Approaches to the Study of Party Organization* (Columbus, Ohio, Merrill).
Wright, W. E. (1971), 'Comparative Party Models: Rational Efficient and Party Democracy', in Wright (1971), pp. 17–54.
Zolo, D. (1992), *Democracy and Complexity* (Cambridge, Polity).

INDEX